Historical Perspectives on Infant Care and Development

Historical Perspectives on Infant Care and Development

AMANDA NORMAN

BLOOMSBURY ACADEMIC
LONDON • NEW YORK • OXFORD • NEW DELHI • SYDNEY

BLOOMSBURY ACADEMIC
Bloomsbury Publishing Plc
50 Bedford Square, London, WC1B 3DP, UK
1385 Broadway, New York, NY 10018, USA
29 Earlsfort Terrace, Dublin 2, Ireland

BLOOMSBURY, BLOOMSBURY ACADEMIC and the Diana logo
are trademarks of Bloomsbury Publishing Plc

First published in Great Britain 2022
Copyright © Amanda Norman, 2022

Amanda Norman has asserted her right under the Copyright, Designs and
Patents Act, 1988, to be identified as Author of this work.

For legal purposes the Acknowledgements on p. xi constitute an
extension of this copyright page.

Cover design: Jade Barnett
Cover image Floral Carpet in honor of Gustzv Klimt on June 17, 2012 in Genzano,
Italy © Alessandro0770/Alamy

Bloomsbury Publishing Plc does not have any control over, or responsibility for,
any third-party websites referred to or in this book. All internet addresses given
in this book were correct at the time of going to press. The author and publisher
regret any inconvenience caused if addresses have changed or sites have
ceased to exist, but can accept no responsibility for any such changes.

A catalogue record for this book is available from the British Library.

A catalog record for this book is available from the Library of Congress.

ISBN: HB: 978-1-3501-6845-9
        PB: 978-1-3501-6846-6
        ePDF: 978-1-3501-6848-0
        eBook: 978-1-3501-6847-3

Typeset by Integra Software Services Pvt. Ltd.
Printed and bound in Great Britain

To find out more about our authors and books visit www.bloomsbury.com
and sign up for our newsletters.

CONTENTS

FIGURES

ACKNOWLEDGEMENTS

Thank you to my sister Pip Taverner who has been able to offer her support and read my chapters, sharing her perspectives and specialist areas about women and healthcare from the past. I also express gratitude to Abigail Gosling and Julie Beams for their professional and social conversations, during some gorgeous food, when I was the external examiner for the BA (Hons) Early Childhood Education, at the University of Bedfordshire. Furthermore, I acknowledge all my Froebelian colleagues and friends, past and present, as well as the women who shared their experiences, inspiring an alternative historical perspective about infant care. Lastly a big thank you to my husband Philip Norman, alongside my four children Xavier, Pandora, Cassius and Lola, who have all been patient and encouraging, supporting me throughout this book project.

Introduction

This book explores infant care from a historical perspective and is organized into two sections, initially considering infant care received at home. The second section of the book then focuses beyond the home and discusses infant care approaches between professionals, parents and infants. The two sections are headed as:

- Part I: The infant at home
- Part II: The infant beyond the home

Each chapter introduces a historical lens about pregnancy, parental relationships, professional's role and some of the services that were available to infants. Within each chapter there are contemplative questions provoking further thought about contemporary care practices. Case studies and practice examples also invite additional reflective discussions. In understanding the discourses of infant care, it is framed and contextualized within early childhood education and care (ECEC), but with a greater emphasis on the care perspective.

The overall intention of the book is an opportunity to submerge into a world of caring for infants, from conception to three years of age, assimilating and appreciating the magnitude of this transitional period of life. I am conscious of the interplay with terms between infant and infanthood in scholarly research. Infant is therefore defined as a living being and infanthood as a shifting of ideas. In reviewing children and childhood, this book studies both the interpretations and biographies of infant care. It examines the relationship between mother–infant relationships and to a lesser extent fathers, alongside the role of associated professionals, from pregnancy to early childhood. This is discussed from a micro- to macro-level in understanding infant care. Therefore, I will be reflecting on the historical discourses and relational interplay between infanthood, infants and infant care. This will include the close maternal and professional roles associated with infant care. Political landscapes will be weaved in, whilst simultaneously including micro stories and biographical studies of families. The aim is to create a more intimate and subjective understanding of infant care, enabling the reader to delve deeper into an understanding of past lives. By exploring infant development and care examples of personal narratives and case studies, it provides the arc for each connecting chapter when evaluating the relevance to today's practice. Rather than presenting social history in a chronological and linear way the focus is on historically contextualized topics. In contributing to the literature and narratives I have drawn specifically on the work of Linda Pollock (1983), Ann Oakley (1981), Margaret Llewelyn Davies (1978), Helen McCarthy (2020a) and Cowan (2021) as sources of insight and guidance within this book. Hugh Cunningham (2017) observed childhood as being readily accessible within portraits, books, literature, advice and fiction, located within a time and place. In drawing on various materials, I have been able to reflect on the cultural attitudes and practices from a community and societal perspective.

Predominately the book is geographically situated within England and Europe, although examples have also been included beyond the West. The aim and purpose for the reader is therefore to appreciate and adopt a cross-disciplinary approach, beneficial to those professionals working with infants today. This may include working and caring for infants in educational, social, health or care contexts. There is often a focus and interest towards the older child and education more broadly in studying early years, with topics including formal schooling, policy and practices. The aim for this book is to further contribute to the early years' field with an extension towards infant care. This book therefore is recommended as an educational and general resource for those wanting to understand more about the origins of infant care practices.

Themes that re-occur throughout the chapters:

- Financial: constraints and challenges
- Lack of knowledge and mixed messages regarding advice of parenting
- Personal intimate relationships between the mother–infant relationships
- Professionals caring for infants
- Infants cared for beyond the home

In recent years the regular caring of infants and young children has been increasingly sought within and beyond the home, with many parents in the west seeking professional care as they return to employment or opt to share their childcare. Subsequently many professional settings who traditionally educated children beyond two years have expanded their group care.

They provide the option of 'baby rooms' facilitating a service to enable the inclusion of infants within their settings. It is therefore considered a timely addition to understand and value the historical context of different relationships and care between infants, parents and professionals.

A broad range of themes included in the book navigate the reader towards specialist subjects and concepts. The topics of the book aim to illuminate material circumstances and how these have changed over time. This includes understanding the present by making some sense of the past. Consideration of how families were constructed and the continuity or re-emerging of ideas and philosophies to caring attitudes towards infants will be examined through:

- contextual research and stories
- social history
- oral evidence
- local and the personal narratives through a biographical lens

In studying the historical perspectives, the reader will be able to explore the following quality assurance benchmark statements of The Early Childhood Studies Degree Programmes in England within the book.

- Reflect upon a range of psychological, sociological, health, historical and philosophical perspectives. Consider how these underpin different understandings of infants and young children and childhood (first section of the book).

- Integrate ideas and findings across the multiple perspectives in early childhood studies and recognize distinctive early childhood studies approaches to relevant issues (second section of the book).

- Evaluate competing positions in relation to the construction of infants and young children and childhood by different subjects, societal agents and time, place and culture constructively critique theories, practice and research in the area of child development (first section of the book).

- Critically explore, examine and evaluate the significance of the cultural, historical and contemporary features of various policies, institutions and agencies in regard to babies, young children and childhood (second section of the book).

- Demonstrate and reflect upon a range of psychological, sociological, health, welfare, educational, cultural, philosophical, legal, historical, political and economic perspectives, and consider how these underpin different understandings of babies' and young children and childhood, nationally and globally (throughout).

- Demonstrate the ability to give voice to and where appropriate act as an advocate for babies and young children, families and communities (throughout).

(QAA Early Childhood Studies Benchmark Statements, 2019:9–10)

Terms

Infant(s): Used consistently rather than 'baby' as a generic term when referring to under three years, with a focus on the first eighteen months.

Infanthood: The period from conception to three years.

Babies: Used in case studies and specifically those infants under one where clarity is needed beyond the term 'infancy'.

Early childhood: Infants under three.

New-born infants: Birth to one month.

Young child/children: The term given to children between two and three years unless otherwise stated.

Care: Providing attention and attending to the needs of health and development through a connected approach.

Carer: The term given when discussing parent, primary adult carers of infants and practitioner as a shared voice.

Gender: Although exploration of discourses about gender diversity are beyond the scope of this book the authors position is gender inclusive. Therefore, narratives are included by those identifying as mother, father, female, male.

FIGURE 1.0 Barbara Hepworth, mother and child, 1934. Pink Ancaster stone Purchased by Wakefield Corporation in 1951. Photography by Jerry Hardman-Jones © Bowness.

PART ONE

The infant at home

CHAPTER ONE

Historical reflections and contemporary practice

Introduction and context

This chapter will explore the relevance of learning about the past, enabling the reader to critically reflect and think about current concepts of early childhood. The rationale for this chapter was inspired by my own teaching of historical perspectives to students as well as their individual interests in researching pioneers. On occasions I have been fortunate to deliver sessions about songs and lullabies with infants. Many students recognize the more familiar finger rhymes and the connection to language and speech development. However, fewer students knew about their origins and significance. This provided opportunities to discuss emotional relationships and the benefits of singing and signing. Friedrich Froebel (1782–1852) was also introduced as a key pioneer and his philosophies about Mother Songs (first published in 1844) as well as how verse depicted everyday life for children. Students became increasingly aware of past connections to their everyday approaches with young children. This sparked an interest to the origins and significance of other contemporary practices and how time periods within society shape attitudes and approaches of infant care.

Significant time periods

By introducing historical perspectives, the British industrial revolution (1815–1860), whilst a few years later than Europe's industrial revolution, is generally a familiar period in history with significant changes occurring and impacting infant care. It was a significant time in the shifted perceptions of cultural norms and the way individuals lived together in society (Cunningham, 2017). Views about children were transformed regarding their contribution to the labour market and the way childhood was perceived as a separate space to adults. The Industrial Revolution also brought about legislation, in relation to the protection and rights of child and a growing awareness regarding public health. This contributed to the improvement of health and well-being for young children, including infants (Marten, 2018). The twentieth century then led to an increased focus on child development as a scientific discipline. Studying children also widened with the emerging use and accessibility from photography to moving picture. Film was developed as a way of clinically observing and micro-analysing behaviour (Evans, 2013). This enabled psychologists and anthropologists a method by which they could utilize to study, present and share their theories about children, including infant care. Reliance was previously on static images, statistical data and narratives in conceptualizing their contributions to understanding children development. The twentieth century was often referred to as the century of the child and an important shift regarding the deeper and scientific understanding of childhood and the child in the West (Kehily, 2013; Key, 1900). In England, organized religion was increasingly questioned by individuals regarding its influence on daily family life, values and practices. Family life was also being de-constructed during this time, and consequently blended families and women were acknowledging and resisting their position in a patriarchal society. Movements such as the ethical society were gaining traction, and families, including wives and mothers, were seeking alternatives about morality and family life beyond the church (Anderson, 2007; Goodall, 2020). Women were writing novels about strong, independent females and increasingly about having children out of wedlock and living financially independent lives.

Today we live in a digital era and this revolutionary technological landscape creates new questions about the society we live in, the comparisons with other societies and how agency of voice is promoted and listened to. Frameworks that determine child, childhood are situated through an ethical and political lens with the accompanying values and rationalities of a given society (Moss and Pertie, 2002). It is therefore important to recognize there are shifting landscapes in the West to an understanding of child, childhood and the current conceptualizations about their meanings throughout history (James and Prout, 2008). Critically analysing how these re-conceptualizations have occurred encourages thought about the meaning regarding the present day of childhood studies. The history of childhood also encourages a rethink about the conceptualizations of agency, identity formation, generational consciousness and subcultures and their relationship with mainstream culture (Wright, 2015). Exploring infant development and care within the broader perspective of infanthood a connection between the psychological and social, the domestic and the public, the past and the future is established.

> *A practitioner's reflection can surface and criticise the tacit understandings that have grown up around the repetitive experiences of a specialised practice and can make sense of the situations of uncertainty or uniqueness which they (practitioners) may allow themselves to experience.* (Pollard, 2005:7)

Contemplative questions

Reflecting on time periods,

What period is generally considered when thinking about historical perspectives of infants and young children?

Why is it valuable to know about infant development and care from the past and what purpose does it serve in contemporary practice working with infants today?

Fixed or fluid in studying infants?

'The past is like a foreign country: they do things differently there' (Hartley, 1953:1). The way historians write and evaluate childhood from the past evolves with time, and as a result there are differing interpretations to how children were perceived and lived from birth. This is primarily because history presented and recorded is not the absolute truth but an interpretation on who is recording it and what they are recording (James and Prout, 2008). The experiences of the infant and the conceptual notion of infanthood continue to create contradictory dialogues, and this is often dependent on the discipline of the writer and the area of childhood they support or dispute (Mills, 1999). For many readers of childhood studies today there is an agreement of childhood being a social construct, culturally shaped, as well as understanding and learning children through a maturational, sequential lens. Therefore, discourses remain disciplinary and contextually focused (Southgate, 2000). Although as a human we have a biographical entity, an embodiment of self, we are also governed by social patterns of culture. Therefore, definitions of childhood can vary depending on the biological or social focus (James, Jenks and Prout, 2004). Within these broad frames there are also different concepts of childhood across geographical space, cultures, time and place. Such disagreements and changing perspectives are the essence of a historical enquiry in understanding health, family's education, care and parenting (Derricourt, 2018; Mills, 1999).

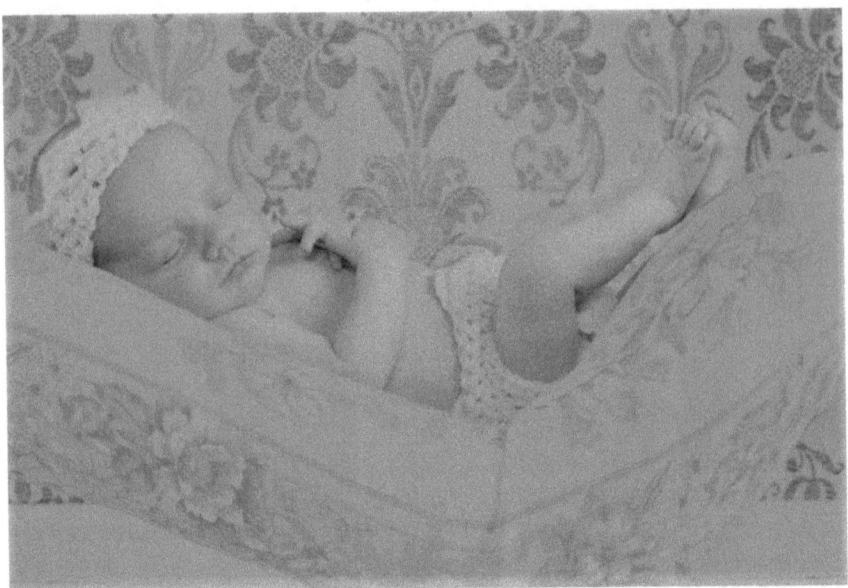

FIGURE 1.1 Studying infants and their care.

Rationale for studying infants

Much has been written about the history of childhood from an educational perspective with a focus towards learning, discipline and school. These are all considered valuable topics to be discussed within and beyond the academic realms of childhood programmes. Infancy is generally included in these discourses but arguably to a lesser extent. More recently neuroscience confirms infancy is a unique period during the life course. Infants experience life through everyday actions and sensations, dependent on their needs met by caregivers. Epigenetics is also contributing to a deeper understanding about nature with nurture (Barlow, 2018). Ideas about care giving are also diverse. This includes shifting from an adult-centred view, who are not worried about their offspring and distance themselves from their infants, or a child-centred view where parents tend to focus all sense of time and energy towards their infant. For many carers nurturing infants is generally the space between these polarized attitudes. These two broad attitudes and therefore approaches to infant care have dominated child-rearing practices for as long as the last 3,000 years, responding and reacting to the social conditions of the period (Coles, 2015). In today's Western culture, protection, time and care are devoted to infancy alongside the financial investments in care, commercially and digitally.

Cultural history is vast in its domain, encompassing beliefs and values about human rights, morality, marriage and family, war and peace, love, and death (Horn, 1994). Cultural beliefs about infants are important because it reflects how society responds to practices and the way care is approached and nurtured. These are often consistent with the culture's attitudes to a responsible infant/childhood and adult citizenship. Bronfenbrenner's (1979) ecological systems theory evaluated how infants are embedded in networks of sociocultural processes and institutions that have both direct and indirect impacts on their development. Bronfenbrenner defined four levels of system functioning around the individual, the infant:

The *microsystem* is made up of all the relationships between the person and his or her environment in a particular setting. For example, all the transactions that take place between the infant and the physical and social environment of the family form a microsystem.

The *mesosystem* includes the relationships between the major settings in which infants are found. An example would be the interaction between the family and nursery.

The *exosystem* extends the mesosystem to include other social systems that do not contain the developing infant but have some effect on them. This may include neighbourhoods, media, local government, economy or transportation that impacts family functioning.

The *macrosystem* contains the various subsystems, beliefs and values of the culture or subculture. It is concerned with the regulation of communities and social systems (Bronfenbrenner, 1979).

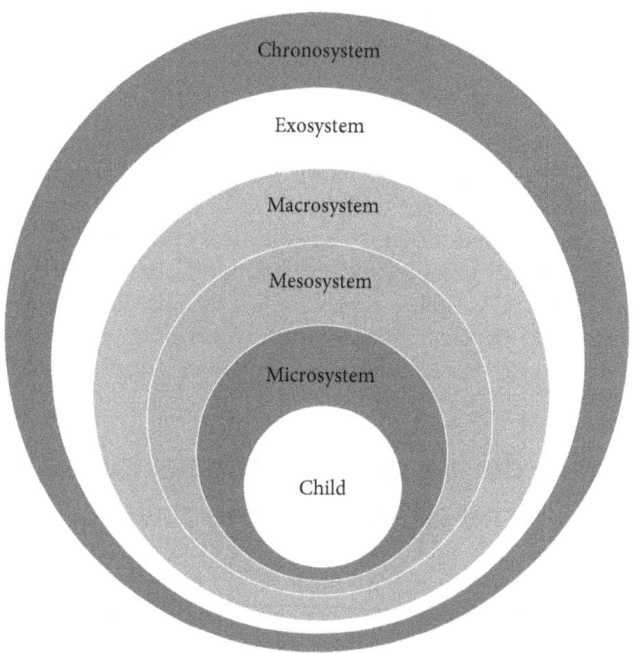

FIGURE 1.2 Bronfenbrenner's ecological systems theory (adapted from Johnston and Nahmad-Williams, 2009).

Each of these systems has a micro history that is embedded within the larger history of a society. The culture of infancy, at any specific period in history, can be thought of as a complex set of relationships between and within each system. In viewing the historical perspectives within this model, it highlights infant development and care shifts through time in relation to the individuals and organizations around them within a cultural context (Celebi, 2017).

Contemplative commentary: Voices from the past

By listening and reading micro voices from both past and present, we gain a sense and understanding to the wider cultural experiences of a given society.

> I often listen to my parents and grandparents tell us about how they bought me up and this has influenced my own practise although sometimes I am really shocked by their stories and cannot believe this was actually advice to be followed!! My Grandmother used to tell me how she would strap my Dad to a pram at 18 months, sitting up and then take us to the garden with toys to play with as she left and went about her work. She remembered and recalled a time when my dad had got stung by a bee and had been crying for some time before she had realised. She said she felt really bad, but it was normal to leave children in prams unattended in the garden while the mother was busy working in home. (Anon: 1950s)

Researching the history of infants contributes and promotes an academic interest, stimulating enthusiasm and interest to historical debates. It encourages active engagement with both the practice and nature of history, and an assessment of the theories and arguments presented by historians of childhood and infancy, through practical explorations and lived experiences. In this way, history becomes tangible and relevant. Infant/childhood is a constantly shifting concept with conceptualizations and theories layered over previous assumptions, findings and practices (Marten, 2018).

Where do we go for information about the child from the past?

The study and research of the history of childhood is considered a developing area in discipline and popularity. Since the translation of Aries's *Centuries of Childhood* in 1962 into English (Aries, 1962; Wilson, 1980), the focus of researchers has moved beyond the 'improvement' of childhood and engaged in a multi-exploration of experiences. This includes the diverse focus on the micro-history. Micro-history is not simply a process concerned with the minutiae of history but is rather an approach that attempts to express and unpick the reality of individual lives lived through research (Brody, 1967; Landecker, 2006). There is also the motivation to represent all forms of history, giving further voice (female perspectives or those from working classes) to those who have been arguably ignored in traditional historical representations (Roberts, 1995). Writing Lives Archives including the Burnett collection about working-class autobiographies, held at Brunel University London library, provides a window into the stories and memoirs about the everyday experiences and identity of the ordinary and extraordinary from the past.

Contemplative commentary: Voices in the present

We often talk about how history has shaped our understanding of the past however I tend to focus primarily on 20th century theories and broad areas such as the development of nature and nurture debates. I would like to explore more about topics such as the history of nursery's or nanny's or day to day living but do not know where to start, I often find these restricts my research – a student voice (Anon, 2020).

Contemplative questions

The following questions provoke discussions and thoughts about studying historical perspectives and how this can be approached by the novice researcher.

What type of history do we want to find out about?
Where do we begin in our research?
Do we want to find out about statistics or the micro study of lives?
What would we like to know more about?

To understand infant development and care beyond the perhaps more familiar twentieth-century scientific historical period is to apply a cross-disciplinary research, including geography, socially, anthropology and education. Sources including artefacts, stories, visual representatives, digital sources, surveys and statistics all build a picture about what life could be like for an infant from the past. Early civilizations studies, biological anthropologists, bioarcheology, examining the skeletal age, social, physical age can provide information about breastfeeding, weaning, diet, physical activity and general health

(Derricourt, 2018; Orme, 2001). Nevertheless, it is important to remember that it is a representation of life as an infant because there is no evidence from the infant themselves and therefore interpretations are relied upon. The closest to understanding infants is to view them from their primary carers and connect their experiences about how infants were portrayed and cared for. Anthropologists in their ethnographical approach have also contributed to research, gaining everyday lived experiences in a culture perhaps beyond their own upbringing. Through detailed data collection the ethnographer can contribute to a wider understanding about different communities and how they live (DeLoache and Gottlieb, 2000). Auto-ethnography also provides a further analysis including and reflecting on the 'self' within the cultural context and society lived in. Examining the minutiae of customs and beliefs, as an insider researcher can be advantageous, observing and micro-analysing the interactions of infant and carer to evaluate a sense of the infants' perspective. Their extensive and often longitudinal studies about infant care and development from the past within and beyond Western societies can therefore be understood from a variety of research perspectives (Wright, 2015).

Heywood (2017) evaluated the many ways history of childhood has been explored. These have ranged from:

- Burial sites
- Medieval coroner reports
- Census
- School attendance reports
- Employment
- Autobiographies
- Photos
- Portraits
- Games
- Folktales
- Songs
- Letters

Pictorial records

One of the influential historians of childhood in the post-war period was Philippe Aries (1914–84) who in 1960 published a French, then translated into English, book: *Centuries of Childhood* (1962). He argued childhood was largely lacking during the Middle Ages, although there was a distinction between infancy (0–7 years) and childhood (7–14 years) within the medieval period (Wright, 2015). However, for Aries these divisions had little meaning in everyday life and once an infant was mobile and communicated verbally, they immediately became a part of the adult world, with little room for what he termed sentimentality in parent–child relationships. Children were regarded as economically useful rather than emotionally rewarding and this was believed to be, in part, due to the high mortality of infants. Infants were therefore thought to be treated with indifference until the end of the fifteenth century. Subsequent views eventually shifted towards a more familiar and modern understanding of the family, with consideration and emergence of the child as an exclusive phase (Cunningham, 2017). Aries (1962) was a demographic historian who wanted to understand the modern phenomenon of childhood and family life better. He identified his research in the historic study of young children's clothes and their demeanour by observing many portraits and paintings alongside official reports including statistical data (Hearn, 2020). One of the issues regarding this type of investigation is that like some forms of written records they were often representations about wealthier members in society. Furthermore, rather than painting realistic images they were generally representations and interpretations by the artist or narrator commissioned by families. By studying paintings Aries considered that childhood did not exist in the sense of how we understand it today. He was, however, careful not to assume there was mistreatment of children with no childhood and agreed some affection could have existed but argued the child belonged to adult society rather than exclusively to their mother. One of the criticisms of his conclusions was that emotions in the past tended not to be recorded, represented or expressed (Retford, 2006). However, this is not a determinate to its non-existence, and many of the intimate relationships from the past between parent and infant were simply unrecorded. It was also argued by focusing on imagery in paintings a misguided representation was also possible. Images were often considered not to be of a child or even the artists' impression but stylized to represent an image of Jesus Christ. Therefore, an infant is often seen with an adult face, particularly in the 1300s (Cunningham, 2017). Internationally secular paintings of everyday family life and portraits of individual children were also less frequently commissioned because of religious faith and in Islamic and Jewish traditions. This was related to the Ten Commandments regarding prohibition of images. However, by the 1500s whilst there remained religious connotations in the images, a much more naturalistic look of an infant was beginning to be depicted. By the seventeenth century there became distinctions between the adult and infant images portrayed in paintings. In Renaissance art infants were much more realistic, with infants even playing with toys (Hearn, 2020; James and Prout, 2008).

Consequently, the absence of childhood could be a misrepresentation to how infants and young children were publicly portrayed.

Departing from painting as a source of historically understanding infants was Pollock (1983). Her research remains insightful because she studied parent–child relations and presented primary sources, by using autobiographies and dairies kept between 1500 and 1900. She deviated from the often relied upon sociological approach in gathering sets of data to infer an understanding about how life was lived within a family context. Her findings brought a fresh focus to the family voice. It was a valuable contribution to the generalizations sought from the larger data sets such as parish records about live births. Her contributions reflected on the emotions as parents and the rationale to their feelings. She disputed the notion of parents being emotionless and distant from their offspring. She therefore disputed Aries's findings regarding the term 'sentiment', although there is an agreement that some of Aries's analysis and terms regarding sentiment were skewed in translation. For example, Aries defined sentiment as an idea, although some of his followers, including Stone (1979), advocated an emotional attachment to the term.

Pollock (1983) used personal documents to build her arguments in the research of adults and children diaries autobiographies letters and wills. She gathered findings from:

- American diaries
- British diaries
- autobiographies
- unpublished manuscripts.

Whilst considered by some as only representatives towards middle classes, her research provided further evidence about ordinary and unexceptional everyday lives of individuals in families autonomously (1983).

However, whilst Pollock and Aries are unique in their approaches to understanding infants in history, they both relied on representations of childhood, pictorial records and written accounts through memories of parents.

Dissemination about family life, from families themselves, passed from the oral to the written tradition also provided a valuable source. However, published material led to an agenda in higher levels of control from those with the means to print their words, arguably creating a literate elite. The printed word on a large scale separated those unable to read, the educated and those with school experience. This often led the illiterate having to rely on interpretations and observed practices within their personal experiences (Postman (1994). This also contributed to the challenges of obtaining authentic views beyond those often already known in the public domain of a society. However, reliance on print such as reading those who published emancipatory narratives or advocating 'better care' remained a worthy medium about how infants were cared for (Baxter, 2011).

Valuable sources in 'building' a knowledge about historical infant development and care: Parenting advice books

Parenting books are not a new phenomenon and have been written by eminent midwives and associated church members for centuries and therefore are a valuable source in understanding the historical development and care of infants. Today we seek to explore information and advice from professionals, from other parents and available websites and popular parenting books. Whilst infants remained constants the advice about them has certainly changed in history (Hardyment, 2007). Reliance on extreme and extraordinaire advice in baby care manuals continues to exist, even though there are inconsistencies between the dominant narrative in manuals and the voices of parents, especially mothers. Childcare experts have their own beliefs and characteristics, cuddly or strict in their outlook on care and how it should be managed. Moreover, a gender bias and consideration of male advocates in the past have also dominated the professional voice around infant care. Middle-class bias also existed to those more affluent with the luxury to ponder about childcare. Being able to contextually understand historical advice is a vital step towards asserting opinions as to how parents want their infants to grow up today (Heywood, 2017).

Contemplative commentary

By approaching historical perspectives there are various ways to begin.

'As a childhood studies student I want to know more about a specific area in relation to the history of infant sleep but there's so much to find out I am not sure where I'm supposed to go' (Anon, 2019).

It is important to maintain a critical approach and to question what is being presented within the documents exploring when analysing primary and secondary sources. The source will need to include an understanding of its place in context and the bibliographical material Cunningham (2006). Historians gather a range of sources to substantiate their claims through a secure grasp of historical context and questioning lenses. It is from this type of approach that narrative, descriptive and analytical techniques are combined in understanding the past rather than relying on anecdotal or opinionated ideas of the past.

Contemplative commentary

We often have a picture of what life was like in the past – mum at home, leading the family care and dad the breadwinner going to work, with the family reliant on his income. Perhaps we visualize doom and gloom with little leisure time or the infants being continuously funny and joyful with few family worries. However sometimes our ideas about the past are not always consistent with the evidence and consequently research and reading are important in broadening our own perceptions.

Learning from contemporary historians and their research

Helen McCarthy (2020) focused on the twentieth century and studied how many mothers worked, although not necessarily in paid employment. In her findings women have always worked, therefore contradicting the portrayal of the breadwinner family, the household, headed by a male worker who was earning a satisfactory to good wage. Earning a wage through secure and skilled work to keep his wife and children was an aspiration that many men did not always achieve. The reality was that many women often worked in numerous ways, unrecognized as an economical contributor to the family home. As women's work around the home remained unacknowledged the ideological power of the breadwinner continued to perpetuate throughout twentieth-century British society. In reading the narratives of women a cultural history of working motherhood, as well as social and economic one is explored in subsequent chapters. Broad narratives of historical change move into sharper focus through the lens of the daily lives regarding women's relationships with their husbands, their work and how they cared for their children. In reading the minutiae stories about family life we can begin to understand and critique the complexities of infants throughout history and go beyond the generally held assumptions about family life.

Learning from archives

Archives are like treasure troves with resources capturing key historical times. They are an accumulation of historical records, accessed copies through new media and physical facilities in which they are located. Archives contain primary source documents that have accumulated over the course of an individual or organization's (Kehily, 2013). Public records and archival material in the public domain are helpful in exploring infant and childhood.

Some useful archives for studying childhood include:

- The National archives
- The Community archives
- The Co-operative heritage
- The Children's Society national archive
- Oral history archives
- Foundling museum and their archives
- The Children's Society
- Mass Observation Study
- The Froebel Archives.

Public reports and population studies

Official documents such as court records, coroners' reports, obituaries and literary sources can further contribute to how infants were cared for at a given time. Wills and last testaments all offer contextualized understandings to how families lived, and infants lives within this. In organizing the way infants have been explored categories have been helpful in thinking about the type of data collecting. The following gives a few specific examples about how research can be organized when researching a historical aspect of infancy (Anderson, 2007).

Using statistical data

- Family resource survey
- Population studies
- Adult reflection/recollection

Biographical research

- Oral history
- Film and interview

- Narratives and diaries
- Imagery

Using literature

- The use of fairy tales
- Fantasy stories
- Novels
- Magical realism genres

(Wright, 2015).

Contemplative commentary: Voices in the present

By reflecting on the chapter so far, an example to the process of embarking on researching of a historical topic is outlined.

Tom is developing a research proposal about outdoor play, specifically risky play and being left with no supervision. He wants to find out if children between the ages of two and three years played in this way in the 1800s.

A scoping review approach is a good starting point in finding out the existing literature, study designs and other sources of information to inform the study.

- Consider how far in history you may want to visit; in this case is it the nineteenth century and would you like to explore it from an international or local lens?

- Are there any specific organizations or relevant play theorists during this period?

- Do these sources have further links and specific go to readings?

- What archives would be helpful?

- If you want to gain a 'voice' in your research would oral history, be helpful in exploring this and would you seek those who have experienced outdoor play from older generations?

- If you explored a different historical period, would the research themes be very different?

Contemplative questions

Outlining a chronological time frame can be helpful as starting point to a particular topic being researched.

What key historical aspects would I find helpful to study further or link to my practice with infants?

As a historical gallop what key times are of interest to myself as an early year's educator and encourages me to explore further?

European historical times can be organized into four key times. These are:

- Early times – the classical Ancient Greek and Rome times, the medieval period of AD 400-1500.

- Late Middle Ages. Medieval of the AD 1500 onwards.

- Changing times/Early Modern times/Transitional times of colonization 1700–1800 with the beginning of the Industrial Revolution. The long nineteenth century (1789–1914) depicts a progression of ideas and a time of mass urbanization.

- Modern/recent times of 1900 to today (Cunningham, 2017).

Writing archive-based histories of children and childhood which covers any period apart from the modern period is challenging because there is a reliance on surviving material. National, local and institutional archives for the premodern era mostly relates to matters of administration justice and finance with little information about children and childhood before 1800. From the early sixteenth century all births, deaths and marriages would at least should have been recorded at parish level. Therefore, there is the possibility of researching the numbers of infants who were born and died at a given time. However, history tends to be detailed within the world of the adult. Therefore, prior to the 1800s children were often only featured when they were recorded as living in institutions, when there had been a death or if they had been taken away for specific reasons (Heywood, 2017). From the nineteenth century the contextual focus of upbringing children and growing interest in how children, including infants, lived began to merge as part of the historical discourse.

A historical gallop of the changing times and infant care

From an evolutionary perspective all humans are descended from a small population of hunter-gatherers who first appeared in Africa during the Pleistocene epoch. The Pleistocene lasted between 1.6 million and 10,000 years ago. From this time humans gradually abandoned nomadic patterns and occupied permanent settlements, developing agricultural living. Hunter-gatherer societies first appeared about 100,000 years ago and were descended from a long line of other human species that were considered to have arisen from the beginning of the Pleistocene (Derricourt, 2018).

By about 35,000 years ago, hunter-gatherer (*Homo sapiens*) groups existed in most locations and during this period were predominately considered to consist of small groups of about twenty-five humans. They existed by hunting game and gathering wild roots and plants to eat. They would not typically travel far, and it was rare to encounter another group. Generations lived their lives within this small sphere of people and place. As expected, artefacts or other documentation of their infant care practices was not left to develop an understanding of this time (Wenke, 1990). Internationally there is some controversy about whether surviving hunter-gatherers of recent times are aligned to the prehistorical hunter-gatherers regarding the similarities to how they live. Therefore, there is a constant interest by anthropologist, historians and those specialists wanting to understand more about societies (Hrdy, 1999a).

From an evolutionary psychological perspective, the *environment of evolutionary adaptedness* was a term devised by John Bowlby (1907–90) the founder of attachment theory (Bowlby, 1969). As suggested, there is no evidence of humans living in large-scale societies until 10,000 years ago. Therefore, this is one major defining feature of environment of evolutionary adaptation. It means humans adaptations were suited to small communities and therefore survival practices such as keeping the infant physically close and creating a bond to protect and feed their infant, like Bowlby's theory of attachment, were possibly practised (Badcock, 2000). The present-day !Kung bushmen, a hunter-gatherer group living in the Kalahari desert in Africa, have been observed extensively and women also continue to carry their infants continuously in a sling and feed on demand, similar to the past (Konner, 2005). However, other present-day hunter-gatherer cultures have been observed to be less protective of their infant and allow substitute care whilst they work. Furthermore, micro-observations have shown attachment styles to be less consistent than others in terms of care (Hrdy, 2009; Mead, 1954). Although not entirely consistent with hunter-gatherer groups, infant care in prehistory could be potentially interpreted as a bonding experience, promoting attachment and developing an awareness of other human bodies from feeding warmth and touch (Devore et al., 2019).

Greek and Roman civilizations

The Greeks were prized for their democratic civilization (600 BCE to 322 BCE), and it was a time of Aristotle, with Greece being a collection of some 1,500 separate cities. Infant mortality was common during this time, so infants were not named immediately (Hearn, 2020). There were two ceremonies to welcome wanted babies into the household. These occurred:

- 5–7 days after birth
- 10 days old.

Greek and Roman (200 BCE–CE 300) literature revealed harsh caring practices with little affection. Athenian infants were swaddled with the aim of straightening their limbs. Infants were generally swaddled so tightly in a bid to mould their bodies and therefore their character as a worthy contributing citizen (James and Prout, 2008). Heads were also pressed to mould their shapes, and cold baths were routinely administered to ensure they did not become too soft in character (Cunningham, 2006). Whilst the care towards infants was considered harsh and cruel to today's societies the Romans believed this was an expression of love, considering their behaviour would evoke the growth and development of strong individuals, physically and mentally. In literature affection towards children was evident as they became more independent and expected to contribute to household chores. However, as well as doing chores there is evidence to suggest toys and games were played and encouraged in Athens. Written evidence also revealed nurture and love existed as well as protecting infants in Ancient Egypt and Greece (800–200 BC) (Cunningham, 2017). Gendered distinction was underpinned in Greek society, and houses included male and female quarters with children under seven living with their mothers, enabling sibling bonds. Physicality was important and unwanted infants' (often females, malformed or compromised health) mortality was assessed according to their sex, a preference to males. Infants were considered the property of the parents, and thus, the head of the family made the decision if they should live. This was continued through the Middle Ages and thereafter (Orme, 2001).

During medieval times childhood was less obvious, their values of the time were different to present day and the child was viewed as an unimportant difference to that of the adults. Their character was formed by the church and, once they were baptized, they were viewed as free from original sin and therefore received into the church. Therefore, from a religiously dominated society infants were considered imperfect and sinful from birth (Baxter, 2011).

Late Middle Ages: Fifteenth century onwards

The puritan discourse viewed children as inherently evil and needing discipline to keep away from evil tendencies. A godly household was an essential requirement for order in the church and in the state as religious views were adopted (Sommerville, 2014). The Old Testament tended to look more favourably towards infants and regarded them as a gift from God rather than parents' property. Thomas Hobbes in the 1600s was concerned with the power and the nature of social cohesion and the social contract. For him the relationship between parents and their children was not about having infants but rather how they lived. It was therefore the father who ultimately made the decision about how their infant would be reared. For him children were not necessarily evil but had little value during the period of infancy. This discourse highlighted how infants were perceived and cared for in contrast to the Middle Ages (Hendrick, 1997).

From the seventeenth century Locke (1632–1704) considered infants were born as a blank slate with no innate knowledge, these being acquired through sensation and reflection, a blank slate on which anything could be written. Therefore, the romantic ideas of freedom and happiness combined with the empiricist ideas of reason and realism saw the rise of value in the individual. Locke believed infants were not born evil but had potential evil if they were born into a corrupt life. It was the guidance and raising of the infants that was important, and this was predominately though education. Indulging them will affect them negatively, and he believed children operated by experience (Locke, 1690a). This included reflection and how children organized their own memory to make sense of information. Locke concluded the experiential basis of knowledge was based on the senses and reflection which led to further complex ideas. Locke therefore considered infants were not born with innate understanding but had the capacity to understand the world (Locke, 1689). Therefore, through experience and reflection children would develop abstract thoughts which lead to the development of reason.

Changing times – transitional times – colonization 1700–1800 industrial revolution

In contrast the nativist Jean Rousseau's principles of childhood were embedded in his writing the philosophical child called Emile. This was considered an educational treatise about the place of the individual in society and Rousseau's understanding about childhood and infancy. Rousseau contributed towards the Enlightenment period and believed infants were born innocent and good (Rousseau, 1762). For this reason, Rousseau stated that it is the society and culture who easily corrupt children. Rousseau emphasized key aspects were formed by freedom, virtue, self-reliance and happiness. The infant is born learning 'before he can speak or understand' (Rousseau, 2011:85). Their senses and their sensory experiences are the 'the raw material of thought' (Rousseau, 2011:91). He believed adults should not interfere with their sensory experiences but allow infants space and time to experience things through touch. This was contradictory to Locke's thinking that emphasized the importance of adult guidance in developing reason in children.

Infants should have the space to grow strong and be free. Through overprotection and 'swaddling' adults were restricting their infant from freedom (Rousseau, 2011:29). Rousseau described that the natural course of child development should not be manipulated by the adult, and this was quite a departure to how infants and children were previously viewed. Childhood was viewed as a separate phase of life, with an appetite for self-discovery as they grow and develop reason.

The eighteenth century was therefore about new ideas regarding childhood. Human life, dignity and freedom were beginning to be valued. A shift of consciousness known as the Enlightenment was emerging and Rousseau (1712–78) at the heart contributed to the philosophical ideas that children were essentially good from the time they were born, widening representations of the infant (McNamee, 2016).

Victorian Times

From the beginning of the nineteenth century a modern era began to dawn. During industrialization poor working-class families increasingly moved to the cities for factory work and even the middle classes were continuing to work in harsh conditions. The state of the local authority began to take a keen interest into the upbringing of children as the new perspective of childhood developed, distinguished from adults and therefore protected from physical hard labour (Humphreys, 2010). Unfortunately, the industrialization period re-conceptualized childhood from the Enlightenment period once again and during this period viewed even the very young as an asset and part of the labour force (Hardyment, 2007). Poverty, ill health and poor housing were also significant features of this period, alongside a developing awareness of sanitization, mortality rates and the links between health and the environment (Hendrick, 1997). As the modern welfare state grew the second half of the nineteenth century resulted in attention being paid to child labour, with the campaigning for child workers to be abolished. Written records, forming archives were developed, alongside records of health clinics schools and charities. This enabled the accessibility of gaining an understanding between this period and today, linking changing legislation, with the rights of the child and family experiences. Prior to public health, poor sanitation and bad diet meant the mortality rate for children was high. Legislation was key during this time and improvements, as well as attitudes to health became a public concern. Technology and science moved into the twentieth century and renowned individuals such as Darwin (1872) and the child study movement once again reconceptualized an understanding of childhood and the child.

The child study movement

Recognizing child development as a particular way of thinking about (or constructing) childhood was influential in re-defining infants and the care received. Besides informing the treatment of children, at home, hospital and childhood centres development concepts have become the everyday language associated with children. Knowing the age and stage of development enabled young children to be understood within a childhood life phase. The influence of the infant development approach was to understand not just childhood but child development and later promote childhood rights. This was viewed as positive in the value attached to scientific-based theories of development. Paediatric medicines and childhood disease became a separate branch. The 1901 Foundation for Society for the Study of Disease of Children developed the medicalization of children, and they were measured and monitored in relation to their health (Higginbotham, 2017). Development psychology also provided ways of thinking and organizing children, and during this period an almost disproportionate attention to infants rather than older children was the focus (Kehily, 2013).

Exploring non-Western societies also supports and invites questions to the way we think about infants from the past to the present. In India, for example, the breakdown of the ages of the 'childhood period' begins at conception and focuses on development stages such as attribution of a name, first outing, their first solid food eaten or ear piercing. There are little concepts of ages and highlights the assumption of child development being a Western viewpoint. Life cycle events are often celebrated and such events of birth, the first hair cutting, marriage and death are the main ones that are commemorated. Gender remains significant and birth celebrations for daughters are more muted than for sons and are sometimes absent altogether. Although India was once led by a woman prime minister, Indira Gandhi, and Indian women currently hold a wide range of powerful positions in every walk of life, there is a strong cultural bias towards males (Hays, 2015).

The history of childhood encourages us to rethink what we mean by agency, identity formation, generational consciousness and subcultures and their relationship with mainstream culture. Childhood is the missing link between the psychological and social, the domestic and the public, the past and the future. The changing history of childhood is commonly viewed from perspectives with deep historical roots.

Connections with contemporary care practices

This chapter introduced the types of historical research that may be less known. It can be quite daunting studying the historical perspectives of early childhood and infant development, especially beyond the key recommended books of a programme. Many readers may feel the twentieth century is the key historical period to focus on with the development of science and psychology. However, understanding the changing landscape of infancy beyond this time is insightful in appreciating how some practices and ideas have remained or been revived during different time frames. It is also worth remembering that listening to older generations, whether family members or visiting a care home, forms part of an oral history and can enrich and contextualize different topics. Similarly, whilst we know portraits in the past were generally commissioned and therefore 'set up' images of the family by those who can afford this luxury, it remains a useful window of interpreting the past. Visiting museums and galleries can be insightful and helpful in gaining a better and deeper understanding about how infants lived in the past. History is not a neat, conclusive subject, but in exploring the past it can shape how we think of the present and therefore inform our future about infant development and care.

Conclusion: A personal note

This chapter considered the way history has been studied and organized as an academic subject. It has included the value of studying infants from the past and how this has influenced contemporary thinking. Rather than a social history book, with assumed previous knowledge of history as a discipline, it draws on the range of material available to the novice historical researcher. It therefore presents an introduction to the different ways and how infant history could be researched and with the types of research that are accessible but often unknown as a way of studying childhood. I wanted the chapter to appeal to a reader with little knowledge of social history as a discipline as well as those more familiar. Archival research is a growing area familiar to those studying childhood, and this chapter invites a broader understanding of the availability offered for further focused research or links to practise.

CHAPTER TWO

Transitions to parenthood

Introduction and context

Early years professionals and practitioners meet parents in a variety of contexts during and after pregnancy. This may be perhaps in the home, a health clinic, a support group, a nursery setting or a social services organization. Therefore, collaboration can often occur prior, during and after birth in a variety of ways and places. Relationships are usually developed between the partner, father, grandparent or another primary carer closely connected to the infant who the practitioner or professional would regularly meet. By exploring pregnancy experience from the past this chapter invites the reader to reflect on rituals and beliefs that have informed understanding about contemporary relationships and practice. Positive relationships between practitioners and parents have a significant impact on infant development, with infants dependent on their care and support. They are the first point of cultural and personal reference points when it comes to infant's socially interacting with the world. Today we know that these relationships can begin before birth and as Music (2016) illustrates,

> The foetus is its own being, with its own rhythms, urges, biological expectations. It's arrival transforms the mother's body into an effective host, and once plugged into the uterine wall, it basically fiddles with its mother's control mechanisms, leading some to liken it to a cosmonaut in charge of a spacecraft. … It has feelings, responds to painful stimuli by turning away and has demonstrated a surprisingly clear capacity for choice. (Music, 2016:14)

Transition to parenthood

Throughout the eighteenth and nineteenth centuries parents had various motivations and external influences regarding the involvement in the courtship of their growing children. Daughters would often go and live with or near their parents in law until they were elderly. Dowries also provided marriage opportunities for siblings, so intervention by families was also encouraged where there was a financial or commercial alliance to be made by marriage (Anderson, 2007). Throughout this period the marriage alliance was often used by commercial classes to keep property in the family (Hardyment, 2007). This was resolved by marrying their first cousin or providing finance for business enterprises (Anderson, 2007:36). Community events were organized with the aim of securing future marital relationships. These included the village dance which was important for peasant and rural labourers in many parts of continental Europe until the mid-nineteenth century. The middle and upper classes sometimes held more formal rituals such as chaperone events, supervised by the elders, as well as placing press advertisements of available dowries (Anderson, 2007; Coles, 2015).

Even though childbirth remained a private and predominately female affair throughout history, being pregnant was rarely a private matter (Pollock, 1983). Pregnancy impacted on families, friends and the community in many ways, including the symbolic representation given by society. Pregnancy within a marital relationship was perceived as social stability, linking to material wealth, property, with virginity viewed as the ultimate respectability of an unmarried woman (Hearn, 2020). The eighteenth century was considered an influential crossroads in history, recognizing the continuing desire to have children, but less of them (Heywood, 2017). One interpretation suggested that sectors of the population whose life chances were not controlled by property inheritance or had a need to build up capital or set up a business had always been less sexually inhibited. Subsequently in the eighteenth century rates of illegitimacy may have resulted from changes in attitudes or from changes to the social context whereby pre-marital and courtship took place (Muir, 2017). However, generally marriage remained an expected and important rite of passage for women as they entered adulthood in Western society.

Ages of marriage

From the seventeenth century until the late nineteenth century Western Europe had a marriage pattern with the typically mean age for rural areas:

- 27 or 28 years for men
- 25 or 26 years for women.

Between 1600 and 1850 there is little evidence of any systematic or patterns of significant change although Wrigley and Schofield (1983) suggested slight age fluctuations for women, although for men the age of marriage remained constant from the eighteenth to the mid-nineteenth centuries.

The highest rank of society may be married at puberty, but generally throughout the population it was later in life, with only 2 per cent before 17 years (Hearn, 2020).

After 1850 and as late as the 1930s the average age for an English or Welsh woman's first marriage was still around 25 years with men being 27 years. This seemed relatively old when the average age of marriage was 22 years and 24 years in England during the 1960s and in the 1970s (Anderson, 2007; Oakley, 1981b).

Christianity and pregnancy in England

Within the West the conception and birth of infants were often viewed as being part of Gods will. In the Old Testament Eve declares in sadness children will be brought forth. Religion, specifically Christianity in the West, undoubtedly influenced the attitudes towards pregnancy and childbirth.

FIGURE 2.1 Visitation of Mary (Rogier van der Weyden, 1440–5).

In early modern Europe pregnancy was often seen and experienced in the context of the New Testament narrative, the visitation (Kehily, 2013).

Visitation was described as the visit by the virgin Mary who was pregnant with Jesus to Elizabeth who was pregnant with John the Baptist. Visitation was a popular symbolic belief in the late fifteenth and the sixteenth centuries, and numerous representations were produced in England when Catholicism was prominent. However, with the introduction of the Protestant Reformation during the reign of Henry VIII (1491–1547) the removal and destruction of Catholic images resulted in few medieval paintings and sculptures existing today. The few that survived visually depict the visitation, the two women portrayed together pregnant. The value of the symbolic representation regarding pregnancy suggests it was perhaps an inspiration for early modern women. It was frequently illustrated in prayer books and other sources. The visitation was also a subject of many sermons addressed to and prayers written for early modern Britain women with their infants (Marshall, 2009).

The first published anthology of English women's writings was *The Monument of Matrones* (1582). It was an anthology of prayers and meditations written for and by women, published in London, England. It was one of the earliest and largest national books and included 500 pages of prayers and meditations. The book included extracts from the Bible and brief lives of biblical and other high-esteemed women. It was organized into seven sections, with four, five and six relevant to women's lives from being a girl, a mother and then a widow. Section five was specifically related to childbirth and labour with prayers, and again the visitation was referenced (Atkinson and Atkinson, 1991; Hearn, 2020).

The visitation had a revival and reappeared in Britain during the nineteenth century onwards, through the works of artists and poets such as the Pre-Raphaelite Brotherhood in 1848. This group was reacting against the narratives of the time as typified by the style of works shown at the Royal Academy. Even in the twentieth century there was still a presence of the religious tension. In 1926 a bronze female figure by Epstein was renamed 'A Study' simply to avoid controversy (Chamot, 1964). The visitation continues to be recognized in terms of its symbolism and in 2003 an English painter worked on a large-scale visitation altar-wall image at the Trinity Chapel, Liverpool Hope University.

Whether a religious interpretation, a symbolic image or an artistic portrayal, numerous pregnant women have been depicted repeatedly in the form of the visitation. The value of exploring the paintings of women pregnant throughout history is the alignment to British women's Christian faith and contextualizing the conception and birth of infants, viewed as matters of Gods disposition. Predominately a life of prayer, sermons and devotional readings were part of women's everyday life and routine. It was also linked to women's concerns of perceived and actual threat about mortality and childbirth, surrounding the life event (Hearn, 2020).

Contemplative commentary

In the twenty first-century Western societies have become more secular with lower rates of church attendance, baptisms and Sunday school attendance. However, a sense of experiencing pregnancy and the connections to spirituality is often referred to as a part of the childbirth experience. Therefore, while many consider themselves atheists (a non-believer), religiosity, spirituality and humanism remain part of the pregnancy, childbirth and parenting dialogue. (Athan and Miller, 2005)

Today religion, including Christianity, is often part of the pregnancy and childbirth discourse and a valuable area to reflect and consider when working as a professional with pregnant women and families.

Health and understanding about the internal occurrences of becoming pregnant

Today conception and pregnancy experiences are influenced by expectations the parents learned through their own upbringing and professional medical advice. Factors such as parents' age, health, marital status, religious belief, social status, cultural expectations and employment circumstances are influential within the parent's community and social norms with conception care and the growing foetus.

Up until the eighteenth century and the introduction of the microscope the male and female genitals were often imagined as identical parts but rearranged. Males' genitalia were on the outside whereas women were thought to be folded inwards. In 1671 Jane Sharp wrote the male genitalia function was "The Vessels that prepare the matter to make the seed, called the preparing Ves I sels." A woman was "The Yard, that from these containing Vessels, casts the seed prepared into the Ma I trix" (Sharp, 1999: 6). In other words, the vagina and uterus were basically an inside-out penis, with testes and ovaries rearranged. It was thought both had to produce a seed if conception was to occur and this would only be successful with an orgasm. Within wedlock it was assumed couples were eager to have children and being childless was as much of a concern than the labour itself (Hardyment, 2007). As pregnancy was often thought to be a gift from God ways to promote fertility lingered into the late and early twentieth century. Fertility was often perceived as the women's responsibility and therefore her duty in continuing the blood line (Hearn, 2020). Alongside mandrake and laudanum suppositories, women also relied on holy relics as well as prayer to avoid infertility. The missionary position was favourable in the two seed belief of procreation. If conception occurred in the morning this would result in a boy whereas conception in the evening would result in having a girl. Thistle juice was also considered beneficial for the womb with lean meat and salt avoided during pregnancy (Heywood, 2017).

During the late seventeenth century differences between male and female genitalia were understood as being unique and the egg of a woman was to be shaken into life by the sperm if conception was to be successful. This supported the passive role women played in sexual reproduction. The accurate diagnosis of pregnancy remained uncertain in the seventeenth century until the 'public' gradual realization that mensuration was linked to pregnancy. There was also uncertainty about the gestational period and the egg was thought to contain a fully formed infant from the outset. Foetal development was therefore thought to be a matter of enlargement rather than development (Pollock, 1987). However, physicality of the foetus was only part of the discourse. Ensoulment, the point where the soul enters the person, recognizing the beginning of life and personhood was understood by the lived-in societies moral, ethical and legal standpoints. Narratives about the soul entering the unborn infant have dated back to Greece philosophy. Early writers from a Christian belief continued to debate the principles and timing of ensoulment. In Christian and Jewish beliefs, it was believed to be the time of conception, when God breathed in the spirit. In Islamic belief this has been debated as being from conception to forty days. In other religions the unborn infant's soul was the reincarnation of another. Indigenous peoples of Australia believed the spirit resided at five months when the infant was felt moving (Crowther and Hall, 2018).

Irrespective of the religious beliefs around ensoulment, pregnancy in Western societies was viewed and treated as comparable to a disease until about 1750. In understanding the body and its changes Humoral medicine was predominately drawn on. This began in Ancient Greece and continued in popularity until the late nineteenth century. The humoral theory was a system of medicine detailing the makeup and workings of the human body, adopted by Ancient Greek and Roman physicians and philosophers. The humours of the body were based on the belief that the body was composed of four humours (temperaments). These were black bile, yellow bile, phlegm and blood. They were also influenced by the individuals' environment. Hippocrates linked each of these humours to one of the four elements of earth, air, fire and water and two of the qualities hot, cold, wet and dry (Carter and Codell, 2012).

Following the humoral system the management of a woman's blood levels was associated with the success of their pregnancy and the way they perceived themselves and their own body. In managing the balance of the humour (blood and other bodily fluids) bloodletting was common practice (Pollock, 1987). The aim of bloodletting, withdrawing blood was about preventing or curing an illness and disease. Bloodletting, either by leeches or by a physician, was considered to have been one of the most common medical practice performed by surgeons from antiquity until the late nineteenth century, a span of over 2,000 years (Cohen, 2018).

Modern medicine has replaced much of the old practices and pseudo sciences. In 1543, medical practices were challenged by a Belgian professor,

Vesalius, determined there were more than 200 errors in Galen's description of anatomy. Furthermore, he considered that much of the ideas had not been based on observation of the human body but from dissecting animals. As the scientific revolution of the seventeenth century dominated, older ways of thinking were gradually replaced by theories arising from observations of reasoning (Fulton, 1950). The scientific method finally paved the way for the future, although it took a further three centuries before clinical physicians with overwhelming evidence disregarded the theory of humours (Sherwin, 2007).

Often perceived as a medical condition childbirth was often approached with little confidence even up to the twentieth century. An uncomfortable pregnancy was often met with fear as the labour drew closer. Hazards such as infections, haemorrhaging and eclampsia were grave concerns, and there were no effective methods of pain relief. Many mothers feared their childbirth because of the risk to themselves and their unborn infants' life, so in addition to arranging nurses, midwives and clothes, a period of mental preparation was also reported in the event of death. This impending fear contributed to why many women resorted to religious and beliefs as a way of accepting the outcome of their birth experience (Pollock, 1987).

By preparing for the practicalities and environment surrounding childbirth the upper classes were able to afford materials such as drapes of white silk around the room with a fire lit throughout the labour. Wooden trays, bowls prepared and sheets and pillowcases, cloths and bandages were all available during the birthing event. For others less fortunate and with little money they had simply to manage with what was available to them (Hardyment, 2007). Rituals such as the closing of windows were undertaken to ensure no draughts were present, alongside the belief it kept out evil spirits. This was known as the suffocation method (Heywood, 2017). It often resulted in a stifling environment and by today's standard poor hygiene practice. The time of labour even up to the early twentieth century was consumed with emotions regarding the risk of death, so much so that it was not unusual for mothers to write baby biographies. In the early seventeenth century, a mother's advice book was written by a group of female authors as a way of recording their future wishes for their unborn infant. The contents of the *Mother's Legacy Texts*, from 1603 to 1713, were left to instruct their children and future carers in the event of death. It was ordered chronologically by the date of the first edition of each advice book and limited to works attributed to named mothers (Heller, 2016). Elizabeth Grymeston was one of the entries, including advice to her only surviving infant, first published in 1604. Even though listings indicated there were nineteen editions made of *The Mother's Blessing* before 1640 very little is known about the women. The first edition (1616) included a woman named Dorothy Leigh. She was described as a gentle woman, identified a widow, not long deceased, and her letter was dedicated to her three sons.

Elizabeth Clinton's advice was dedicated to her daughter-in-law, addressing mothers nursing their own children, something she had not personally done. Elizabeth Brook Joceline composed her Legacy about how she would like her infant to be brought up if she died, whilst awaiting the birth of her first child, having become convinced that she would die in childbirth. She did die nine days after the birth of a daughter, in 1622 (Harde, 2002). This was possibly the most poignant of the mother's advice books, intended as an instructional advice paper about what to do with her forthcoming child and how she wanted them to live their life. However, all the writings were a response to motherhood (Hearn, 2020; Lell, ND).

Contemplative commentary: A voice from the past

Within Pollock's (1983) research findings we are able to gain a sense of the mother's voice during this period. Elizabeth Stirling (1816) writes to her husband:

> My dearest husband as it may perhaps be the unerring will of God that your wife should die in giving birth to her child, I feel it an incumbent duty to address a few lines to you on the most important subject. The care of the soul of our infant on your own external interests ... we all need pardon which God is willing to extend to us for his blessed son, we all need holiness of heart and life which is also received through him. I beseech you my dearest husband to impress these saving truths early on the soul of our child. Let the world word of God be the daily study of both.
>
> (Pollock, 1983:29)

The concern at childbirth was often about saving the mother. However, this changed with William Smellie (1697–1763) a Scottish obstetrician and medical instructor considered to be one of the first prominent male midwives in Britain. He designed an improved version of the obstetrical forceps, establishing safer delivery practices of the time. Smellie challenged the commonly accepted concept of saving the mother in preference to the infants during times of birthing complication. Through the introduction of forceps in the field of obstetrics, he was able to carry out more delicate movements, and had the ability to resolve life-threatening circumstances surrounding the mother and infant when complications arose. He was also the first recorded figure to be able to resuscitate an infant after lung collapse (Leap and Hunter, 2013). Irrespective of the dangers to pregnancy women continued to strive to have a family. Pregnancy, as a temporal state, was as much a biological condition as a cultural one.

Connections with contemporary practice: Faking pregnancy or a fashion statement?

In 1793 there was a short-lived fashion and chimes with some of today's sweeping fashion statements when it comes to showing off a pregnant abdomen. In recent years we have seen tops become shorter with the proud display of tight flesh, floating dresses with high-cut waist bands and side-ruched tops to emphasize the pregnant figure and shape. However, in 1793 an unusual attire became popular, in the form of what was known as the belly pad. These were pads that deliberately gave the impression of a pregnancy without being pregnant. This wasn't the first time women were presenting a pregnancy shape with many fifteenth-century sculptures and paintings depicting what looked like a pregnant figure. In fact they may have simply dressed to give the impression of being pregnant by others. This was a look considered between the time of 1561 and 1636 and perhaps with mortality rates high and a desire to respond to speculation. The pregnancy look, predominately within wedlock, seemed to be a favoured shape (Hearn, 2020; Rauser, 2017).

The short-lived fashion of belly pads, giving the impression of being six months pregnant, was worn by women attending social functions with a deliberate impression of a 'bump'. It was a popular look and swept London, England, in the year 1794. It was typically a linen bag, the size of a small pillowcase left open at one end with ties or buttons full stuffing. The rationale for the style was thought to allow women some sense of freedom, influencing questions about the sexual knowledge of the women wearing it and their desire of motherhood. However, in further recent explorations regarding the wearing of the pad it has been interpreted as a fashion depicting the neoclassical visual culture of art dress during earlier periods rather than depicting pregnancy. Whilst pictures including satire images made women seem pregnant from the side, from the front, the style deliberately emphasized the wide exaggerated hips. It was therefore argued to be a look similar to the hip pads and bum rolls in the dress attire of the times. Nevertheless, the rationale for the 1794 'look' was short-lived and replaced by short high waist for the next decade, considered a more successful style of fashion (Rauser, 2017). Whilst fashions changed pregnancy continued to be celebrated and concealed throughout society.

The fear of pregnancy, unwed and mortality Infanticide

Infanticide, or the killing of a baby, was punishable by hanging in early modern England. Unlike married women accused of infanticide, the mere fact that single women had tried to conceal the death of their babies was considered proof of murder under the Infanticide Act of 1624. A single woman's only recourse was to try and prove that their infant was stillborn, and they had not killed it, a challenge when many births had no witnesses. In the mid-eighteenth century, many women were accused of infanticide with a high proportion being employed as servants and under the age of 16 years. As the century progressed juries found more women innocent rather than guilty of infanticide, unless it was proved they had murdered their infant (May, 1997).

The case of Elizabeth Turner highlighted the fear and shame single women felt when they became pregnant and the lack of privacy in their lives as servants. She did not speak at her trial; instead, witnesses for the prosecution were called initially before the judge and jury and responded to questions about whether she hid her pregnancy and infant. A midwife, an expert witness Dinah Beaven testified that the infant did not appear to have been murdered. Finally, a prisoner in Newgate with Elizabeth stated that they also came across infant items sewn into Elizabeth's coat, when the prisoners took it from her as a bartering resource for food, water or bedding. Elizabeth was therefore attempting to make provision for her infant, and this provided evidence that she did not intend to kill her infant. The court therefore released her.

The transcript to the case depicting the narratives that prevailed during the trial

Primary Source Text: June 1734: Elizabeth Turner, of Clerkenwell, was indicted for the murder of her *Male bastard infant, by strangling it with both her hands, April 12.*

The prisoner was servant to Mrs Windsor, a pastry-cook, in St. John's Lane. I and Margaret Goldsmith, came to lodge there but a little before Ladyday, 25 March, the beginning of the year on the old calendar, and then we observed the prisoner looked big, and at Easter, she looked very lank. We suspected she had been delivered, though she appeared publicly every day. And we had never heard her cry out, but then we could not think what was become of the child. In short, we thought the family was all alike, or things could not be kept so private. We watched and harkened all as ever we could. Once while ... we fancied the child might be at nurse in the garret [attic], because they were often whipping up and down stairs. But when we could find nothing, we concluded it was baked in the oven. At last Mrs. Goldsmith, going into the cellar, came up, and told me and her husband, she had seen a wig-box below, and smelled something. He went down, and came up again, like a dead man, and said, he put his hand in the box, and felt a child, but was so surprised that he did not take it out. We consulted what to do, and, says I, as they have kept this thing in hugger-mugger [secret], we won't let 'em know the child is found before we fetch for a constable [policeman]. So Mr. Goldsmith fetched a constable and watch [man who watched the streets to prevent crimes], and they brought the child up, and it was all mouldy. The prisoner, at first, denied she had had a child; but in a little time owned it was hers.

Juryman: You seemed very diligent in watching the prisoner. Did you ever tax [question] her with being with child, before the child was found.

Elizabeth Windsor: The prisoner never told me she was with child, but she said she had been ill, and had had a great deal of water come from her, and then she was much better. When the child was first found, she denied it, but owned it afterwards.

Dinah Beaven: The child was crowded in the box and putrefied. It was at the full time. I could discern no mark of violence. [There] was a small wound on the head; but I have known such a thing happen to an honest woman's child; when it fell from her for want of assistance.

Sarah Hawke: When the prisoner was brought to Newgate, some of the other prisoners took her coat, for garnish money. And they found these baby things, sewed up in her coat. Here's a shirt, a cap, a stay [a tie for clothing?], a forehead-cloth, and a biggin [a tight fitting cap].

The jury acquitted her (Payne, nd).

The rituals and objects surrounding death have varied across centuries and continents, often revealing how families and infants within a culture lived, how they were perceived and the grieving rituals carried out. An example of this, dating from the first half of the second century CE, was a Roman marble coffin. It was an expensive funerary item created to commemorate the death of an infant. It depicted an infant, in the arms of a parent riding in

FIGURE 2.2 Life cycle plaque: Child's life course.

a carriage, on the far right of the stone, with the last scene, signifying death. The torch carved symbolized a funeral, alongside a winged Cupid (Rawson, ND). This highlights the symbolic cultural reference to how infant death was valued.

In the early nineteenth century portraiture also became prominent as part of a consoling artefact and an object of remembrance. These were often paintings of children just before and after they had died. Rather than dismissing infant death post-humus portraits of infants were on occasion commissioned, thought to provide comfort and remembrance during grief (Hearn, 2020). Similarly photographs and keepsakes are treasured today as a remembrance to infants who have died.

Childbearing, mortality and Family Size

Before the late nineteenth century in Europe (although in France it was considered earlier), there was a combination of late age marriage and relatively long birth intervals which meant family size comprised of around six members, although variations of average sizes did fluctuate in some areas. For many fertile women an average of eight children would be born during her reproductive life, with an acceptance that at least one infant would result in miscarriage, stillborn and death in infancy. Therefore, for smaller families, with a small rise suggested in the eighteenth century, the successful outcome remained important (Hearn, 2020). For the family historian, however, it is not just about the reduced number of children but also the changing distribution of having children during a marital life cycle that is significant. During the pre-twentieth-century populations, births were consistent during the whole fertile period. By contrast since 1900 fertility and childbearing have been compressed into the early years of married life. The rationale appears to be because individuals were living longer and therefore the time for an old age period, with no childbearing, was deemed increasingly appealing. Combined with the age of marriage falling and women having their last child, couples born in the last 100 years have therefore been able to look forward to a period of life as an older couple, free from the cares of bringing up their children. Having an opportunity to live longer resulted in greater economic positions for women and their family. It also creates a new understanding regarding family relationships (Anderson, 2007).

Aspirations: Family composition in England

Moving from family size to family composition the nuclear family has been present since the Middle Ages, with the church dictating rules of conformity about monogamy in marriage. Investment in children was related to their value economically within the family, particularly in agriculture communities. This continued until industrialization and trade textile industries moved the young child from the home to the factory (Sanchez and Lopez, 2018).

In England, as family compositions changed, the cultural context of the late twentieth century was a relatively stable uniformity of life, evolved around visible rites of passage, a cycle of school, marriage, work, retirement. These predominant life aims were generational patterns, providing a moral compass that individuals progressed towards, often adopting a religious framework of life. However, as the political and economic climate shifts with time, so has the navigation of life courses, including marriage, employment and having children. This illustrates how society responds and re-constructs to changing influences, met with uncertainty and new challenges (Sinclair, 2018).

Families themselves are therefore variable, complex and dynamic, and whilst individuals may seek a partner similar in their own background values and beliefs family structures have changed with time. Traditional patriarchal relationships in the family group were challenged in the twentieth century, with increased acceptance of gender equality and resisting the conformity of previous generational norms. Rites of passages were less fixed and with a reduction in religious moral codes and exposure to individuals challenging stereotypes, separation, divorce, surrogacy, adoption and same-sex parents have become progressively accepted as possible trajectories to family living. Whilst it is appreciated that family pluralism is not a new phenomenon, growing tolerance and acceptance for all family types increased in the twentieth and twenty-first centuries. Blended families, the re-forming of existing family groups and creating new ones now define family beyond a heterosexual couple with two children. Parents and families therefore resist and push against generational family 'norms' that previously existed (Palmer, 2010).

Contemplative questions

By connecting an understanding of families from the past to our modern day thinking we should consider the following questions.

Compare your parents with your own marital status. How have things changed?

Have you mirrored your parents' rites of passages?

If you are not married do you consider this a natural progression within in a relationship and are your reasons social, personal or religious?

Do you see marital status as time bound?

What do you think marital status could add to a relationship?

What are the links between marital status and family life, personally, socially and culturally?

Living together as a family

Throughout history size and membership of the household in most Western societies and in preindustrial Europe were relatively large and complex in structure, frequently containing members of more than two successive generations and often including extra members such as cousins, nieces, nephews, aunties and uncles. Today we see families in varying forms, and Wade and Smart (2002:94) categorized families into four types.

- Aggregated families that have seen complex changes and where there are several parents attached to various children within the family.

- The divorced family structure is characterized by small family size and cooperation between parents post separation in comparison to aggregated family's characteristic characterized by small family size and cooperation between parents post separation.

- Meshed families are families with the extended family considered important and children in these families are emotionally literate. Emotions are not suppressed and shared.

- Diasporic families are when a parent has returned to their home country or where the extended family is dispersed (McNamee, 94).

In the second half of the nineteenth century (LePlay:10) described three ideal family types.

1 Patriarchal family. These types of families emphasized stability and authority, leading to a large domestic group containing transcendence of patriarchy

2 Stem family. These family groups were often widespread particularly in Eastern Europe of peasant societies. They also had a patriarchal element, often restricted to the son and his descendants. Other children might remain unmarried in the household with household sizes potentially including as many as eighteen persons constituting as one family.

3 Unstable family. These are often characterised by urban manufacturing populations and in contrast with the other types were often founded by the marriage of two independent individuals during their lifetime. Their children becoming economic investments as soon as they became independent and parents exercised little control over them.

Laslett (1965) suggested that in England there was misconception about family groups and large and complex households were never commonplace. He published an analysis of listings for a hundred English communities from 1574 to 1821. He concluded the mean household size in England had remained constant at approximately four to five from the sixteenth century to the industrialization period. He also concluded the stem family had not been common in pre-industrial England. The evidence regarding household composition data seemed to confirm the view that only 10 per cent of households pre-1821 in English communities only had 3 per cent as kin from beyond their immediate family of husband and wife. However, most households had a maximum of two generations living together. There were a minority containing relatives of three different generations, but it was unusual to contain four generations.

In making sense of families from the past and today a recent turn in sociological studies of the family has been influenced by the work of Morgan (1996) and his notion of family practices. Morgan (1996) advocated considering what a family does, their functionality, instead of what a family is. According to him a family is a quality rather than an entity organized around a set of activities or practices which can create different meanings at different points in time. The potential of this new theorizing of family for the social study of childhood is the inclusion of infants and children in the analysis instead of just focusing on parents. A focus on family practices, as Morgan advocated, enables the conceptual repositioning of infants and children within the family when studying families. Furthermore, Seymour (2007) noted the recognition of family life as being both created and reproduced in the process achieved through the activities and interactions of family members. This included families in private spaces of the home as well as workspaces of the home (McNamee, 2016). The nuclear family could be viewed as a state of mind rather than a particular kind of structure or set of household arrangements. What really distinguished the nuclear family from other patterns of life in Western society, according to Shorter (1976), was the sense of solidarity, separating the domestic unit from the surrounding communities.

The domestic home

Household members in the past were extended to servants in urban areas commonly after 1900 and in London there were often people boarding in the family home. This was linked to the amount of wage earners and from 1850 there was a slow decline of both lodging and service servants in England. The number of live-in male servants was infrequent, and rural-based living in apprenticeship posts was reduced as factory-based industries increased. Female domestic service, however, remained high and was considered the largest single occupation for women in Britain through to the twentieth century, with large numbers still leaving home at an early age in many areas of Europe (Roberts, 1995a). Another contributory factor to the dynamic of family life was the external social controls upon them. Historically social control of individuals decreased in the beginning in the sixteenth century but accelerated again in the late seventeenth and eighteenth centuries. This was frequently framed around societies' religious motivations to control family behaviour and an almost overwhelming concern with family members (often women) morality. Additionally, the involvement in community-based festivals and activities organized reduced and shifted in purpose and the aspirational home space was prioritized as a place to be. Domestic architecture changed from a segregation between rooms for sleeping and eating and conducting business with the introduction of corridors. In the eighteenth century this was particularly important and spaces in the home were created in more affluent families so they could be secure from the intrusion of strangers, as well as the increased segregation of domestic servants from the meals and sleeping apartments. It was associated with new aspirations, particularly by wives for more privacy and defined roles in status to those who worked and lived in the home. By the late nineteenth century there was an emerging culture of home sweet home, although this movement was largely based on their desire to preserve a little self-respect and secrecy in what typically remained a public world of small, overcrowded houses (Ross, 1993).

Contemplative questions

This chapter has provided various facets to family life, how and where they lived. In developing the reading further consider the following questions to reflect and review on some of the topics presented.

- *What does a family community comprise of?*
- *How have family communities differed from the past to the present?*
- *What defines a good infanthood?*
- *What is the definition of a good infanthood?*
- *So how do we think about working with parents today compared to the past?*

Connections with contemporary care practices

Aries (1962) maintained that whilst there may have been more affection in the mediaeval family the institution was not organized in a manner likely to encourage the close supervision of the young family. Life was community life and there was little distinction between public and private, with young children commonly sent away from the family home at a young age to live and work with relatives or neighbours. The seventeenth century witnessed the emerging and increase of a new idea of the effective family. Parents and their infants, children, took pleasure from each other's company and gradually cut themselves off from the outside world. In the modern age traditions and celebrations and festivities became an extension of family life beyond the courtship objective. An example of this is the twelfth-night festivities being replaced by the Christian family 'Christmas' day of today, appealing to parents and young children as a time to celebrate together (Cunningham, 2017). Therefore, there was a shift in the understanding about the responsibilities of (in this example Christian) parents who are now seen as accountable before God for their children's souls and indeed the bodies of their own infants. In turn this impacted on the way infants were cared for. Aries (1962) claimed this led to new ideas about childhood, recognizing the child was not ready for life and that he had to be subjected to a special treatment, a space, a type of quarantine before being allowed to join the adults. Aries believed modern concepts of childhood continued to develop in many forms and was additionally dependent on the class system, with the wealthier merchant and professional classes affording a kind of value system for ideas to flourish. These new varied and accepted way of caring for infants are the ones we recognize in the west today (Kehily, 2013).

Conclusion: A personal note

This chapter looked at the historical way families came together and supported individuals in their transition to parenthood. It included the generational influences and the perceptions about families through religious context and health assumptions. It focused on the perceived and actual barriers in the transition to parenthood. The latter part of the chapter then considered family and family composition in understanding how families were formed throughout history. I wanted this chapter to introduce the voices of those whose circumstances were common of the time in caring for infants, as well as societies' expectations and fashion influencing women and pregnancy. The changing family, viewed through an historical lens, revealed the societal shifts and how this continues today. It is also a timely reminder that families are not fixed but fluid and composed of their actions rather than what they are.

CHAPTER THREE

Parenting and family life

Introduction and context

In recent years, the relationship between parents and their infants has undergone many changes, with parents consumed by conflicting discourses about how to care for their infants. Parents choose whether to be strict or lenient, performance-focused or indulgent. Generally, parenting styles are not an either-or approach, but more fluid about how care is conceived and approached at various stages of infant development. Child-rearing includes advice about feeding, sleeping, discipline and vaccination, to name a few. Medical and cultural advice changes by informed research evidence and policies. This can influence parenting styles and associated attitudes, with those favouring greater emphasis on parental authority whilst others preferring reasoning, following an attachment-led care approach. As parents devote more time to work, a sense of guilt has been known to impact on their parent–infant relations, even though many parents generally spend more face-to-face time with their children than previous generations. These historic changes in parent–child relationships have culminated in diverse attitudes to parenthood and an appreciation regarding some of the past thoughts about infant care practice and relationships (Kehily, 2013).

But what does life inside the womb mean to the baby? The mother is gradually getting accustomed to the idea that there is going to be a baby and the baby is also gradually preparing for life outside. Babies are unquestionably able to survive if they are born at seven months' gestation, and their capacities and reactions are in many ways like a full-term infant. So, we must presume that for the last weeks of pregnancy babies are capable of being aware of what is happening to them. Research shows babies hear their mother's voice, not to speak of father's and siblings' voices; indeed, new-born babies often turn to the sound of their mothers speaking as though they recognised the tones. (Miller, 1992; DeCasper and Fifer, 1980:175)

The arrival of the new-born infant and family life

Cunningham (2017) depicted an infant wash time experience, seated in the bath, playing and making noises in the water. Through the playful clapping of hands and splashing the infant soaked all those around him. His carer then takes him on her knee and begins to play and interact, wrapping him in his swaddling sets. It is a familiar scene to many new parents as they experience bath time with their infant. What is fascinating and strikes a chord was the time the scene was recalled. The scene was depicting Jesus as an infant in the fourteenth century. It was an account by Saint Ida who had been permitted to assist with St Elizabeth during bath time. Whilst we often regard historical bath time a rarity, during medieval times self-hygiene was met with frequent washes and the thought it reduced personal diseases. Whilst the vision was a memory later described in a confession by Saint Ida it highlighted the use of 'utensils' used during bath time and the interactions that occurred between carer and infant.

In Anglo-Saxon cemeteries the buried bones of infants have crumbled away with time but what has been discovered by archaeologists are the artefacts, thought of as toys found alongside the infants' crumbled bones. These have included glass beads considered a play resource. Feeding instruments have also been found and were made in the shape like a breast, perhaps highlighting an attempt to sustain life. Recent sampling methods have enabled an investigation of small ceramic vessels as possibly feeding utensils for infants dated from pre-historical central Europe. Rebay-Salisbury et al (2021) noted that feeding vessels of the past worked in similar ways to contemporary infant feeding bottles. The food stuffs analysed were thought to compliment or provide an alternative to breastmilk. They concluded that during the Bronze Age the vessels provided an opportunity for other members of the community to feed the infant, sharing responsibility of their care and potentially enabling the mother further freedom. This reflects the possible value of parental care in history rather than the assumed dismissed attitude often described (Cunningham, 2006).

Death of an infant during the Middle Ages was extremely common, and this was intensified with infectious diseases such as plagues. However, many accounts in the Middle Ages have revealed a continuation of loving relationships and ways of retaining life and consideration rather than the ambiguous or active denial to the value and responsibility of caring for their infants (Sanchez and Lopez, 2018). This is supported by Pollock (1987), who revealed from sixteenth-century diaries that children were wanted, but descriptions of emotions were minimally recorded, although she did note some evidence of parental emotions conveyed in writings through the death and illness of their infants. During the seventeenth century thirteen parents recorded that they were concerned about the health of mother and their infants being stillborn. They were also reported to be anxious about having too many children. In the eighteenth century further details were provided about the birth as a rite of passage and how it would change family members lives, in both negative and positive ways. In one example during 1889 to 1919 evidence was documented about a father who was not particularly liked by his children or the father liking them in return. Another entry from Pollock's diaries included the harrowing experience of losing a child at three years, describing the death and love felt for their child (Pollock, 1983).

A further example of parental attitudes towards their infants and young children was John Wesley (1703–91), who was a leader of the Methodist movement. He published a paper about his mother, who had raised nineteen children and shared her principles about parenting. Wesley outlined her advice during her funeral, 1 August 1742.

- **Devotions** The Lord's prayer was learnt first, and young children were expected to say it each morning and evening.

- **Routine** A tight schedule was employed in the home. Times were assigned for naps, education, meals and bedtime.

- **Naps** Infants slept during scheduled times.

- **Self-regulation** Self-will was perceived as sinful and caused misery therefore the children were taught to have self-control.

- **Positive reinforcement** Obedience and conformity was required.

- **Forgiveness** A child was never punished for the same offense twice.

- **Peace** Quietness and serenity was advocated in the home (Iovino, 2018).

Contemplative questions

By reflecting on this advice discuss how it chimes with twenty-first-century infant care and parenting.

What would you disagree or agree with Wesley's approach in today's care of infants and young children?
The church was influential in how infants and children were cared and reared. What influences family life and caring practices today?

More recently, in the twentieth century, Oakley (1981) evaluated mothers' accounts during their first few months with an infant in the 1970s. The findings revealed clear divisions of a mother's involvement with their infants compared to the father. The father was recorded as only seeing their infant more frequently at around five months of age in the evening, Saturday or Sunday. Whilst there are many misconceptions around women and work the illusion of the male breadwinner remained during this period. The father's support remained limited in the home care of their infant. Oakley (1981) also considered mother's perspectives towards their new role as a parent. Her findings reported women felt it was monotonous, with just over half of the participants reported as feeling isolated. Many also felt tied down and a high proportion of women felt they had no time for themselves. Overall, just over half underestimated they thought they would find it lonely (Oakley, 1981a). Although this is a small sample and cannot be generalized to represent the whole population in England during the 1970s, the findings do remind the reader of the contemporary concerns around maternal mental health in mirroring some of those feelings from past to present.

Everyday care of touch, cuddling and swaddling and family life

In the twentieth century Winnicott (1896–1971) argued you cannot really describe the infant without their relation to the primary carer as the two go hand in hand. He considered the infant as existing within the orbit of their mother's care. In response to this description, it aids a better understanding about the needs and healthy expressions of the infant's/child's inner world, and their attempt to communicate with their environment.

Winnicott recognized that infants who had a 'good (enough) mother' could flourish and develop, despite a lack of hygiene and physical conditions exposed to, often associated with families deemed to be living in poverty. It was the warmth of mothering, infants being carried, cooed to as well as the sensory experience of skin-to-skin contact that contributed to the close relationship and thriving infant (Norman, 2019). In 1948 Halliday made the link between mortality of infants and touch, acknowledging that infants deprived of maternal bodily contact were more inclined to lose appetite and become physically compromised. Subsequently volunteers were encouraged to attend children's hospitals and provide regular caresses to fretful and vulnerable infants, handling and rocking them. Consequently, this improved the infant's physical health. This approach differed to Wesley's parenting style of scheduled sleep and rigid routines. Winnicott also moved away from caring practices such as wrapping infants up and leaving them for long periods as was customary in many homes (Hayward, 2009).

FIGURE 3.1 Madonna with the swaddled infant Albrecht Durer Date: 1520.

Historical overview of swaddling

Swaddling is an age-old practice of wrapping infants in blankets or similar cloths so that movement of the limbs is tightly restricted. Swaddling bands were often used to further restrict the infant. Swaddling has fallen in and out of favour during the centuries. Swaddling, whilst not as tightly as previously carried out, is once again a popular way of soothing the infant, although medical and psychological opinions about the effects of swaddling are divided. Some modern medical studies indicate that lightly swaddling supports infants to settle and remain asleep in a supine position, which lowers the risk of sudden infant death syndrome (Davis, 2014; Gordon, 2019).

Several authors presume that swaddling was invented in the Palaeolithic period with the earliest depictions of swaddled infants crafted as ritual offerings and grave goods from Crete and Cyprus, 4,000 to 4,500 years old (Coles, 2015).

FIGURE 3.2 'Aztec Cradleboard Figurine and Drawing [Object]', in Children and Youth in History, Item #432.

FIGURE 3.3 'Earthenware Mold of a Swaddled Child [Object]', in Children and Youth in History, Item #215, Susan Douglass.

The ceramic figurine of an infant in a cradle (also called a cradleboard) was created by the Nahua, or Aztec people of Mexico, between 1350 and 1521 CE. It shows how infants were kept bound in a cradle or carried on a cradleboard.

An earthenware mould for casting a figurine of an infant was found in Tangyangu, China, and is likely to have dated between 960 and 1279 CE, during the Song dynasty. The mould measured 3.2 inches long, and this finding highlights the widespread practice of swaddling, or tightly binding the new-born infant with strips of cloth (Douglass, nd).

During Tudor times, swaddling involved wrapping the infant in linen bands from head to foot to ensure they would grow up without physical deformity. A band would be attached to the forehead and the shoulders to secure the head. Infants would be swaddled like this until they reached about nine months. Shorter (1976) evaluated swaddling, which aside from being physically harmful reduced the motherly interaction with their infant. The infant was unable to wave their hands and feet, reach out or grasp any dangled object near them. They were restricted in the bonds and unable to respond to maternal playfulness. If they were tied from their heads to their feet, they could not respond to tickling or clucking, although in Shorter's view this inferred that mothers were probably not doing this anyway. There were no signs that swaddling was significantly reduced until 1850, although there were some reductions of swaddling a century earlier by the middle and upper classes. This was influenced in part by Rousseau, who advocated that the infant should be liberated from swaddling and gain a freedom with their limbs (Shorter, 1976:198). Scientific opinion towards swaddling also began to change, with the association of neglect and swaddling, especially regarding wet nurses and other carers. Often swaddled infants would have been left for long periods, often hung from a nail as women carried on with their work, without washing or comforting them. Concern about infants being neglected, left in their own urine and faeces, was increasingly considered unhealthy (Heywood, 2017). William Buchan (1729–1805) published a home health guide in 1769, and whilst the first part is devoted to preventing ailments through proper diet and exercise, the second part guides families to diagnose and treat ailments, ranging from coughs and hiccups to jaundice and gout. Buchan also showed particular concern for the health of women and children, whom he believed were frequently misunderstood and neglected. He condemned the restrictive infant swaddling. He blamed the high child-mortality rate on upper-class ignorance about child-rearing, with his book becoming a popular health guide (Dunn, 2000).

More attention was also paid to cleanliness and areas such as nappy changing. Locke, in his writings, mentioned potty training and passing of a stool every morning. Another example was in the seventeenth century when Louis XIII began to be toilet-trained at eighteen months and was able to successfully go to the toilet by three years of age.

Cradles also became more fashionable, with the decline of swaddling, and Rousseau believed that a healthy mind could not exist in a sickly body and to flourish the freedom of limbs were essential (Hardyment, 2007).

The child's first sentiment is to love himself, and the second, which derives from the first, is to love those around him. For in his present state of weakness he is aware of people only through the help and attention he receives from them. At first his affection for his nurse and his governess is mere habit. He seeks them because he needs them and because it feels good to have them; it is more like consciousness than benevolence. He needs a long time to understand that not only are they are useful to him but that they want to be useful to him. It is then that he begins to love them. Nature exercises children continually, it hardens their temperament by all kinds of difficulties, it teaches them early the meaning of pain and sorrow. Teething gives them fevers, sharp colics bring on convulsions, long coughing suffocates them, worms torment them, plethora corrupts their blood, various leavens ferment it and cause dangerous eruptions. Almost all of the first age is sickness and danger: one half of the children who are born die before their eighth year. The tests passed, the infant has gained strength, and as soon as he can make use of his life its principle becomes more secure. (Rousseau in Greenleaf, 1978:755; Dutton, 1969)

Rousseau (1712–78) had a far-reaching influence with his ideas about infancy, depicted in the fictitious child Emile. He considered infants were naturally good from birth, innocent but vulnerable and entitled to freedom and happiness. The idea of infants being born 'good' contrasted with the dominant views about childhood of the time (Wilkinson, 2006).

In the early twentieth century, a procedural and 'hands-off' method to caring practices once again prevailed advocated and accepted by parents in caring for their infants. Watson (1878–1958), a popular psychologist of his time, felt the key to success in bringing up a *better baby* was to not overstimulate the love response by giving too much stroking and caressing towards the infant. He believed mothers needed the physical time to fulfil household domestic chores. He evaluated if the child grows to observe attention and distraction from his parent at the expense of household chores then the child would develop an unreasonable affection towards relationships as an adult rather than the necessities and attributes to a successful life (Hardyment, 2007). This chimes with aspects of Wesley's Methodist mother from the early 1700s. Watson considered too much cuddling led to a reduced time in thinking about the science of life and the act of a child occupying themselves, through exploration and engagement. He therefore alluded it was the need of a parent (predominately the mother) indulging their infant. He considered the desire to comfort and touch their infants as leaning towards a form of sex seeking, and in responding to Freud's theory on sexual development was to avoid it all together, eliminating the love factor and the behaviours, that of touch and cuddles along with it. As in previous centuries Watson returned to advocating the treatment of children similarly to adults, with a focus on respect and morals instilled (Davis, 2014).

In 1946 another expert came to the fore with what was considered a more common-sense approach. Spock (1903–98) advocated a gentler approach than previously advocated in the early twentieth century. He invited parents to trust their instincts and encouraged affection and recognized infants as being different to adults. This was a popular approach in the 1960s and indeed followed Bowlby's (1907–90) attachment theory of the 1950s. Bowlby recognized that infants thrived best when they were cared for by a significant primary carer, meeting their needs (Piper and Smith, 2003). The consciousness of the young infant was almost entirely dependent upon bodily sensations emotions and sensory experiences in perceiving the world around them (Freeman, 2016).

Connections with contemporary care practice

Contemporary practice, known as kangaroo care, is the early touch practice advocated, resembling how kangaroos care for their young. The skin-to-skin contact between parent and their infant is considered valuable and contrasts with the often-hands-off approach historically advocated in a bid to ensure healthcare was optimum (Christensson, 1998). Today touch and handling are considered essential, including for those infants cared for in special care units, attached to machinery and tubes where touch is more challenging to achieve. In contemporary society the West is increasingly regarded as a high-tech, low-touch environment for infants. Devices such as bouncy chairs and car seats with prams attached are marketed to ease the physical holding and care necessary with infants. Whilst a hands-off approach chimes from practices of the past, informed research recognizes the value of touch and a hands-on approach to development and relationships. Infants' needs have not changed; rather, it is the cultural advice and expectations placed on parenting that shifts with time (Zeedyk, 2008).

Everyday care of feeding and family life

Feeding

Infant feeding takes many forms, and within the polarized views of breastfeeding or bottle feeding there are many more individualized styles adopted with specialist equipment used. Breastmilk can be given to the infant in several ways, including exclusive breastfeeding, mixed breastfeeding and continued breastfeeding. Exclusive breastfeeding is when the infant receives human milk directly from the breast, and the infant is not introduced to any solid or other liquids for the first six months of their life (Labbok and Krasovec, 1990). What was once universal, and a health necessity, has become a life choice in managing and supporting existing parental lifestyles. Contemporary literature suggests the decision to breast- or formula-feed is entwined with numerous factors, including consumer marketing of formulas, and rather than advocating breast is best feeding, promotion should be focused on normalizing breastfeeding in a Western cultural climate where the choices of bottle feeding are deemed favourable (Norman, 2019). It was not until the eighteenth century that texts on child-rearing activities were written for a feminine audience, and even then, this audience was made up of an educated elite. The earliest direct commentaries were by women (mostly in diaries and correspondence) who complained of the difficulties they were having with nursing. Furthermore, the advice provided was aimed towards sisters, daughters or friends (Knott, 2019; Ross, 1993).

European medical doctors have urged mothers to nurse their own children since classical antiquity, but their advice had little impact on urban populations until the end of the eighteenth century and tended to be restricted to the educated elites and those of the poor with little option (Roberts, 1995b).

> We beg and exhort the most noble women to … (feed) … her infant her own milk, for it is very important that an infant should be nourished by the same mother in whose womb and by whose blood he was conceived. No nourishment seems more proper, none more wholesome than that same nourishment of body that glowed with greatest life and heat in the womb and should thus be given as a known and familiar food to new-born infants … Women ought to consider it best, very honourable, and commendable to suckle their own children, whom they should nourish with great love, fidelity, and diligence.
>
> (Francesco Barbaro, De Re Uxoria, Venice, 1416:16)

Whilst maternal nursing was encouraged it remained the exception rather than the rule for middle and upper classes. Apart from countries in central and northern Europe, where handfeeding was widespread, maternal breastfeeding was largely limited to rural populations and those urban mothers who could not afford a wet nurse. It was also generally the father who made the decision about sending his children out to be wet nursed. From his perspective there were several daily and financial considerations which could easily have outweighed the view of centuries of medical advice about whether the biological mother breastfeeds (Grieco and Corstini, 1991).

Health and beauty

Until the eighteenth century breastfeeding was also viewed by many as dangerous and health debilitating. The higher the rank in class, the more fragile the mother was to breastfeed. The effects of breastfeeding impacted the figure, but more significantly an improper diet and mineral deficiencies could cause hair and teeth loss, as well as a drop in body fat, with scarred breasts. Another barrier was the fashion of the time in wearing a corset. From the sixteenth to the eighteenth centuries corsets were worn by females from about the age of three years during their waking hours. The corsets flattened the breasts and compressed the ribcage. Different forms of nipple shields were sometimes used for protecting sore or cracked nipples. Sucking glasses (used to relieve engorged or inflamed breasts) could also be adapted to draw milk from inverted nipples; the process was complicated and uncomfortable. Therefore, most mothers opted for an alternative, and this was generally a wet nurse. Once again, the social position of the mother would play a determining role in her ability or willingness to breastfeed her own infant (Goodwin, 2018).

Mortality rates were also high and in 1730–79, 50 per cent did not survive their fifth birthday. Breastfeeding was therefore considered an important aspect of survival alongside other milk alternatives. However, there were many misinterpretations regarding breast milk. *Clostridium* was considered poison, so the infant was not fed until the third day when the milk came through (Coles, 2015). The mother's first milk, colostrum, was not considered milk, and was viewed as an unfavourable colour with evil properties. This idea may have been due to the yellowish colour and thick mucus texture of colostrum, which changed to a more accepted looking milk after three or four days. Evidently the infant who was breastfed from the first day by its own mother and who received these important substances had improved prospects of fighting infections during their first week of life. This contrasted with an infant who was fed with the 'older' breastmilk of a wet nurse (Holt, 1921). Sexual relationships during lactation were also thought to spoil the breast milk. Sexual relations were therefore forbidden during the entire nursing period (18–24 months) as it was believed that intercourse would 'weaken and corrupt' the breastmilk. A new pregnancy was also considered to 'poison' the breastmilk, depriving it of its 'substance', so that the nursling would sicken and eventually die. This belief was based on the medical theory of the time. Breastmilk was thought to be menstrual blood purified and transposed from the womb to the breasts and that women only had enough milk/blood to feed one child at a time (Coles, 2015). Simultaneously the prime objective of marriage was to have as many children as possible. Children guaranteed the economic strength of a family and ensured the continuation of the blood line and the family name. They were important in their parents' strategies for social advancement through marriage and business. They were also expected to support their parents and other relatives to old age. The need and desire for children was further increased by high mortality rates, which meant by conceiving approximately twelve there was an increased chance of four to six surviving (Anderson, 2007). Therefore, the use of wet nurses improved mortality rates. Wet nurses were women who had the role of breastfeeding infants other than their own, or in addition to as a form of employment (Knott, 2019).

The practice of wet nursing goes back at least 3,000 years as a form of employment contract to Babylon *c.* 1720 to 1686 BCE. It was a preferred way of feeding Royal infants. Henry VIII had wet nurses, and Queen Victoria had them for her nine children. Wet nurses continued to be employed in households until the twentieth century (Grieco and Corstini, 1991).

Although preferable from an infant's health perspective the use of wet nursing was thought to potentially affect the infant's psychological development. Rousseau had concerns that a profound conflict arose from such practice within the psyche of the child when the child was returned to their biological mother. He was concerned the infant would love the wet nurse more than the mother. They would be unable to distinguish her role as servant, culminating in eventually despising their biological mother. Rousseau believed mothers should be the primary carer for their infants, a notion not considered fashionable for many. Wet nurses' and carers' support was often sought outside of the home, but for Rousseau it was a missed opportunity to what we now consider a valuable period in developing a bond between parents and their infant.

> Does not the child need a mother's care as much as her milk? Other women, or even other animals, may give him the milk she denies him, but there is no substitute for a mother's love. (Emile, 1762:1)

Rousseau (1762) argued the practice of finding 'help' to carry out care roles with their baby instilled a physical and emotionally distant relationship with the lack of physical contact between the infant and parent.

This echoes Stone's (1977) claim about the eighteenth century seeing a transformation in the preferred method of infant feeding, with mothers wishing to breastfeed. Russell (1842–76) spoke about his wife regarding breastfeeding, stating she had a great deal of trouble from their infant not sucking (Pollock, 1983). Most infants were not restricted to any type of feeding schedule, being breastfed on demand. In the second half of the eighteenth century, however, when women of the privileged classes began to nurse their own children, scheduled feeding was recommended by doctors as being more compatible with the mother's social responsibilities, although there is little information on whether this advice was followed. In poorer families, when the women worked in the fields or at home, breastfeeding may well have been restricted to intervals determined by the work schedule. Moreover, alternative substitute foods may also have been introduced early. Similarly, wet nurses who also did strenuous physical work or who had dietary deficiencies could face the problem of an inadequate milk supply. In this scenario they were supposed to return their nurslings to the family, although many were dependent on their financial role and so continued to keep the infant.

The practice of wet nursing remained through to the twentieth century across all social classes and the latter twentieth century documented wet nursing as a regular occurrence among the upper classes. Burnett (1985), in *Destiny Obscure*, included a memoir from the late nineteenth century, which highlighted the acceptance of wet nursing.

I understand that when my sister Alice was a baby my mother's first Lady X also had her first baby. Being unable to feed her baby my mother was engaged as a wet nurse and walked to X Hall three times a day to breastfeed Lady X's baby. She received a meal each time and this she did for three months by which time the baby was sufficiently developed to be hand fed by the nurse. (Burnett, 1985:289)

Today discourses about breast milk and feeding continues. The donation of breast milk is preferable to formula milk for a premature infant, and therefore the donation of another mother's breast milk is welcomed and given to the infants to support their healthy development. Some critics are, however, concerned about the unintended consequences of turning human milk into a product, with the selling of human milk (Gershon, 2015). Wolf (1999) concludes breast milk is an invaluable, morally troubling commodity, dating back centuries.

Contemplative case study

This case study includes some reflections to modern-day breastfeeding and how past generations have shaped their choices. This is a helpful starting point to then discuss the historical aspects of breastfeeding and wet nursing.

Infant feeding preferences and the reasons for parental choice continue to be culturally embedded and generationally bound. Mannay (2016) explored mothers and grandmothers' intergenerational views and experiences of breastfeeding, using visual artefacts and narratives. Her findings concluded that culturally mothers in the twenty-first century still felt under surveillance by the public and their decisions were challenged, irrespective of whether they bottle or breastfed. The use of artefacts alongside their narratives provided a useful way of exploring parents' perspective and one that could be extended to professionals and practitioners in understanding care narratives and decisions made within families (Mannay, 2016).

Weaning

In the seventeenth century, the use of eggs and meat broth began the slow decline in the nutritional value of infant foods. The earlier these foods were introduced the less an infant was breastfed, the greater were their chances of developing health conditions such as rickets, infantile scurvy and bladder stones. The hazards of mixed feeding were also further compounded by a lack of cleanliness in feeding vessels such as sucking horns, rudimentary feeding bottles with cloth teats and long-spouted cans. These tools were difficult to wash properly, and even then, contaminated water could render the most thorough clean useless (Hardyment, 2007; Knott, 2019).

In the eighteenth century weaning was thought to occur much earlier than today's recommendations although in the mid- to late twentieth century British working-class mothers introduced solid food at an average of four months. Over half of mothers also began to wean their infants under three months (Ross, 1993:143). However, the types of food introduced have varied over the centuries. A mixture of flour, breadcrumbs and water was a way of satisfying the infant if they were not feeding (Heywood, 2017). Many seventeenth- to nineteenth-century books on infant care contained detailed recipes for one or several of the following infant foods, pap, gruel and panada (Obladen, 2014). Pap was one of the two main infant foods used for mixed feeding continuing into the early nineteenth century. This consisted of a liquid (usually milk), a cereal or grain, and an additive for flavouring or extra nourishment (such as spices, sugar, honey, butter or eggs). Panada consisted of a liquid (usually meat or pulse broth), breadcrumbs and various additives. Vegetables other than pulses were not used in either of these recipes as they were believed to

FIGURE 3.4 'Phoenician Baby Bottle [Object]', in Children and Youth in History, Item #251, Susan Douglass.

be an 'unhealthy' and unsubstantial food, fit only for the very poor. This weaning pattern continued with cereals such as barley biscuits or groats soaked in water or milk, introduced early in the hopes that the infant would be satisfied after their feed (Coles, 2015). Rural wet nurses were known to introduce the cereal pap as early as three months of age. It was anticipated weaning, introduced when the infant had all their teeth, at around two years of age and nature's sign that the child was ready for solid food. However, unsuitable foods, unsterile feeding vessels and unclean water regularly gave rise to complications, when supplementary nourishment was introduced with nutritional deficiencies also developing over time.

Phoenician baby bottle

A Phoenician terracotta vessel featuring a human face, with the nose forming a narrow spout, was an archaeological find from Carthage, near modern Tunis, dated to 399 BCE–200 BCE. Archaeologists believed it was a baby bottle. Such vessels were known as guttus and were placed with Greek infant burials of the same period, placed near the infant's head. These bottles may also have aided the process of weaning the infant from breast milk to solids (Douglass, nd).

This ceramic cup with a drinking spout is from the cargo of an Arab or Indian ship that sank in the Strait of Malacca between 826 and 850 CE (Douglass, nd).

Pasteurization was the name of the process discovered, in part, by the French microbiologist Louis Pasteur and was the turning point to feeding infants. This process was first used in 1862 and involved heating milk to a specific temperature for a set amount of time to remove microorganisms. There were a couple of different methods of pasteurization, and although farmers may have known about pasteurization, it was unlikely that they would have practised it (Holsinger et al., 1997).

When bottle feeding was popularized amongst the poor it still presented health problems because they lacked facilities for sterilization or refrigeration. The bottles were associated with summer diarrhoea and, although suspected from the 1870s, were conclusive by the early twentieth century. The identification and isolation of the E. coli bacteria in 1945 provided a link to the cause of diarrhoea. The bacteria multiplied through unsterilized bottle nipples or formula and were spread by flies making infants sick. The scientific findings became a national health concern and resulted in public health initiatives, educating families, particularly mothers about the link to health, hygiene and illness. The infant welfare movement campaigned to educate mothers about domestic hygiene alongside sanitary

FIGURE 3.5 'Sippy Cup [Artifact/Object]', in Children and Youth in History, Item #220, Susan Douglass.

conditions (Leap and Hunter, 2013). Water supply, street cleaning and plumbing arrangements also contributed to improved public health. The central aim of St Pancras School for Mothers, founded in 1907, successively the infant-welfare centres, was maternal nursing. They exclusively offered breastfeeding mothers' cheap dinners. Women seeking advice for alternative feeding were expected to provide a medical certificate confirming they were either unable to or had been advised not to nurse. Posters were also designed as visual reminders for mothers about scheduled infant feeding (Rowold, 2019).

The childcare reformer Truby king (1858–1938) was credited with drastically reducing infant mortality in New Zealand, following his enforced approach to breastfeeding, reducing mortality rate, although his style to success was not particularly child-centred. He advocated a parental style of regimes, discipline and detachment towards infants, and these were adhered, in part, by mothers in England. This was perhaps in a bid to obey the expert's professional advice, with advice messages linked to health concerns and healthy behaviours with caring for infants. His follower Mabel Liddiard assured mothers in her mother craft manual in 1928 that feeding at regular intervals would result in self-control, the recognition of authority and later respect for elders (Rowbotham, 1997). Strict regimes of feeding approaches were advocated, and parents were encouraged to avoid touch, placing babies in their own room to sleep, and left for long periods outdoors and as soon as possible, with little interaction. If necessary, an infant was given a ten-minute daily cuddle. The intention was to 'harden and strengthen' the infants, with the regime focused on eating, sleeping and growing, and little consideration of emotions and bonding (Wright, 2015).

Everyday care of sleeping and family life

Historically, sleep practices and advice have varied widely, responding to changing technological, economic, political and social conditions (Bigner and Yang, 1996).

In the eighteenth century sleeping problems became increasingly documented, although early autobiographical entries about sleep concerns existed much earlier. Lady Anne Clifford (1590–1676) was concerned that her daughter would not be able to sleep independently in a bed by herself without her maid. She was worried because her daughter had slept with someone until she was five years old.

Cobden Sanderson (1840–1922) also included a long description regarding sleep with her eighteen-month child. Initially a forceful approach was administered, whipping the infant when all else had failed. Afterwards the infant cried louder and in resolving this she cuddled him tightly and told him to stop and go to sleep. The infant then obeyed what was asked and was able to self soothe both during the day and night independently. The entry then continued with an entry a few months later. The entry discussed how her infant had caught a life-threatening fever. Consequently, following the illness the regime around sleep time described seemed to be less enforced.

It was noted the mother would spend time soothing her to sleep, rather than employing the initial strategy of self-soothing and harsh discipline if disobeyed (Pollock, 1983:122).

Prior to the mid-nineteenth century, sleep was routinely a shared, and for some a public, event. Napping or falling asleep in public places was commonplace (Ekirch, 2001). Individuals shared beds with strangers in public inns, occasionally even those of the opposite sex. Indeed, the notion of rooms designated for the sole purpose of sleeping did not occur until the eighteenth century. Night-time sleep, however, was routinely broken into two distinct night-time periods. The first sleep occurred after sundown until sometime in the night when individuals would awaken, sometimes for a few hours. This time was spent thinking, talking or praying. The second sleep, as it was defined, would then commence until daybreak (Ekirch, 2001). Until the mid-nineteenth century, children's sleep was not a topic of concern or academic enquiry. Child training centred around issues of morality and religion. Regulating children's sleep was a reason neither for concern nor for action, with the understanding infants and young children would sleep as much as was needed in length and time (Stearns et al., 1999). Marie Stopes (1880–1958) in the mid-twentieth century also distinguished between types of sleep, light and deep. If a young infant was left to wake independently from a long sleep, they would be happier and less grumpy and disorientated in temperament (Hardyment, 2007; Pollock, 1983). The turn of the twentieth century brought shifts in attitudes and behaviours relating to sleep and child-rearing (Stearns et al., 1999). Families moved in large numbers from the country into large urban areas. For the middle classes, the economy of the family moved from home-based production into a wage economy, where fathers left the home for employment. This resulted in clearer divisions between male and female roles emerging, fathers 'going' to work and mothers as home makers. This shift to city-dwelling caused many families to live in smaller homes and much closer together. The home was considered a place of safety from street life and an opportunity to create a homely environment as best they could (Grant, 1998). The need for separate bedrooms for the purpose of health and better sleep was encouraged. Experts increasingly urged strength and self-sufficiency through sleep with a designated space for sleep (Stearns et al., 1999). Further, separate upstairs bedrooms led to the need for a sleeping space that would safeguard the infant from noise and assure their safety whilst they slept unsupervised. As a result, cribs in isolated nurseries rapidly replaced cradles as appropriate sleeping spaces for infants. Previously cradles had been portable and were moved to wherever the parent was. Cribs were larger pieces of furniture than cradles and therefore remained in one place, thus reinforcing isolation for infant sleep (Ekirch, 2001). The ability to afford separate bedrooms for children also became a sign of status. It was not until the mid-twentieth century that prams were used and remained a luxury, with the ability to rent them by the hour if they had not been purchased. These were often used as cots and somewhere the infant could be put whist the mother carried daily household chores (Hardyment, 2007).

Another aspect affecting sleep in the home was the invention of the electric light bulb. This altered the relationship to darkness and the daily boundaries set by the rising and setting of the sun (Ekirch, 2001). The invented luminous light impacted on family life, as well as work. Electric light meant that adults no longer needed to retire when their young children went to sleep. The notion of adult time as separate from family time therefore emerged. Parties and other adult-oriented activities could now take place after infants and children were put to bed (Stearns et al., 1999). For adult time to occur, infants needed to be asleep in a separate location for the night. This was an opportunity to create a space for the infants and children separate from the adults within the domestic home. Aesthetically pleasing domains of the rooms were created, with the aid of home decorating books, advising parents on the appropriate decorations, differentiated gendered styles, unique in appeal and distinguishable in space to the adults (Anderson, 2007).

Connections with contemporary care practices

This chapter ends with a focus on sleep practices for infants from birth to three years. Today the overall message for infants is generally an array of mixed messages, with parents seeking advice from celebrity-endorsed books to professional health visiting advice and family members offering anecdotal guidance. This results in the act of sleep being a culturally contextualized behaviour, with huge emphasis, particularly in the West. Professionally the advice in England today is for parents and infants to share a room but not a bed during the first six months of age. Once an infant reaches six months (still often earlier) it is not unusual for the infant to be moved to a separate room and then placed to 'sleep' in a cot, following the parents' routine. In early years' settings day sleep is less forced with 'nesting rooms' designed. These include soft furnishings and neutral colours to create a restful ambience. Cots have been replaced with floor baskets to enable the infant to be able to crawl in and out and reduce the separation of wake and sleep time. The infant can then enter into the basket themselves and wake physically being able to move to and from. This potentially reduces the anxiety around enforced sleep times, with little autonomy from the infant themselves. With the domestic space, artificial light, cultural attitudes, behaviour and social conditions sleep remains a prominent discourse similar to previous generations.

Conclusion: A personal note

This chapter was inspired by the daily lives of families and practices that remain with us today. This includes the complexities of breastfeeding, weaning and sleep patterns. The chapter was informed by a wide range of literature and moving time frames to highlight the topics. Therefore the focus was to present an overview of infant care practices with navigations towards wider readings and specialist topics that may be of further interest. Child-rearing is sought from generational advice, professional understanding or popular parenting book advice. Linking archaeological findings was an aspect I considered an enhancement to the descriptions of practices. Evaluating infant care, it appears to be a continued culmination of what parents chose to listen or ignore, pending their own perspectives in social or religious context.

CHAPTER FOUR

Infant developmental and holistic care

Introduction and context

This chapter discusses the conceptual thinking and understanding about infant development. It does not presume to include an understanding about development in its entirety and selectively focuses on key conceptual shifts within infancy and early childhood. Furthermore, it examines how infant and child development has been historically viewed by parents and professionals. It builds on the notion that development is both nurture and nature and how this influences daily living. From this perspective broader themes and case studies illustrate how families lived in the past. It will therefore contextualize infant development and the challenges they have faced in the past. The latter part of the chapter focuses on the holistic care of infants and was specifically inspired by the narratives captured by women in history. By including these in this chapter they aim to develop an understanding and appreciation of mother's circumstances and the complexities towards caring for infants.

> One of the most powerful influences on development is what happens between people, inferring interacting with children should be at the heart of daily practice. (Hobson, 2002:7)
>
> Children are like tiny flowers; they are varied and need care, but each is beautiful alone and glorious. (Froebel, 1700)

Nature-nurture

The theory of nature-nurture has dated as far back as 400 BCE and Bynum (2002) suggested that Hippocrates described human behaviours as biologically determined. These were the results of four different body fluids. Humours determined individual characteristics and personality traits. Galton (1874) concluded nature was defined by hereditary factors, features activated from genes. Nurture was therefore defined as environmental and external influences post birth (Galton, 1874). Descartes (1596–1650), a French mathematician, scientist and philosopher, was one of the first to formulate the first modern version of mind–body dualism. This was the development of a new science grounded in observation and experiment, viewing the mind and the body as separate functioning entities. Contemporary research now confirms that the mind and the body are not independent but interlinked and interdependent. This is evident through physical behaviours, responses and emotions (Watson, 2021). Pinker (2004) stated nature and nurture should not be perceived as alternatives, but rather a relationship between the two concepts. Behaviour is therefore the result of an inseparable interaction between hereditary and environment during development (Pinker, 2004:3). Nurturing nature therefore encapsulates the influences surrounding developing infants (Barlow, 2018).

Development

Development, according to Locke (1690), was the conceptual understanding that individuals were born as a blank slate. His notion of a 'blank slate' meant that Locke's argument positioned him firmly on the nurture side of the debate. Universally infants were perceived as being a 'blank' slate and, from their first experiences with the external world, gain knowledge from their surroundings. This definition inferred genetics were not significant to development. Although Locke did acknowledge the capacity of an increasing awareness to senses and emotions, as an infant develops and grows, through experiential knowledge. Locke's (1632–1704) image of the infant was therefore tabula rasa, an analogy comparable to white paper, or wax, that could be moulded by those teaching them. This depiction is argued to support a deficit view of the child as lacking and needing to be filled with experiences (Rogers, 2020).

As a polarized position nativism has a history in philosophy, particularly as a reactionary response to the empiricist views of John Locke. A nativist, Jean-Jacques Rousseau (1712–78) understood infants to be biologically pre-programmed. Rousseau argued that children differentiated from adults and should be immersed in nature as a way of learning about themselves and the world around them. By being immersed in nature the infant will grow and develop as a rational, civil and empathetic adult. The philosopher Immanuel Kant (1724–1804) argued the human mind knows objects in innate ways and must experience all objects continuously. In the early twentieth century, Lyons (1970) continued to support the view that infants have certain cognitive functions from birth that allow them to learn and acquire certain skills, such as language development.

Another view was the interactionist philosophies, stressing that both the interaction with the social (family and society) and the natural environment were valuable to development. Therefore, by fostering relationships, nature promotes an infant's innate understanding about the world and their position within it (Cunningham, 2017).

From the mid-twentieth century child development in the West was predominately studied from a maturational development perspective (sequential approach) and included areas of physical, intellectual, language, emotions and social development (PILES) or social, physical, intellectual communication and emotional development (SPICE) in understanding and measuring abilities. Through signposting and plotting milestones parents and practitioners can examine development at an anticipated rate. As a framework SPICE, like a jigsaw puzzle, has influential parts that are important to know as an introduction to thinking and understanding infant development (Music, 2001). Predictable changes in physical functioning occur from birth through uncoordinated and jerky actions to smooth and intentional co-ordinated movements. The infant explores and begins to learn about their physical environment (Macintyre, 2012). Developed and supported by Jean Piaget (1950s) a sequential perspective to understanding cognitive development enables early years practitioners and educators the ability to identify areas and connections of development (Selby and Bradley, 2003). By focusing on the maturational process, an understanding about the growth of the physical body and the progressive abilities of motor skills is accepted and documented (Reed and Walker, 2014). Piaget's four stages of intellectual (or cognitive) development were:

- Sensorimotor. Birth through ages 18–24 months

- Preoperational. Toddlerhood (18–24 months) through early childhood (age 7)

- Concrete operational. Ages 7–11

- Formal operational. Adolescence through adulthood.

Whilst Piaget did not claim his four stages of intellectual (or cognitive) development were reached at a certain age, it was often included in the stages as an indication of the average time frame a child would achieve. Piaget considered the sensorimotor stage (birth to two years) as a time frame when one of the main accomplishments during this stage was object permanence. This was knowing that an object still existed, even if it was hidden. This was known as the exploration and understanding of physicality and cognition through sensory investigation (Barnes, 1995).

Contemplative question

Many readers would have some prior knowledge to child development, and this question encourages the reader to reflect on their own position about development.

Where do you position yourself in understanding infant development and what has influenced your thinking in the twenty-first century?

It is also advantageous to think about holistic development as well as the discreet areas of development. By adopting a purely maturational theoretical

FIGURE 4.1 Louise nursing her child (Mary Cassatt, 1898).

approach to development there is the assumption a controlled sequence of change will inevitably occur. There is also the concern that by exclusively focusing on a maturational approach, surveillance in the achievement of development milestones will be adopted and prioritized when observing infants and children. If the development sequence does not transpire within a time frame and the child fails to achieve, strategies will often be used to promote the sequence of change through a scaffolding approach or more directed style with infants. Whilst this is helpful in making generalizations and supporting infant development it only provides a singular view when thinking about development. Infant development is a rapid developmental phase, influenced by the environment and their physical body from within as well as externally. Illness, medical conditions, opportunities, interactions and external inhibitors can interrupt the milestone approach (Music, 2001). Increasingly an interdisciplinary model of development, referred to as the biopsychosocial model, could be further adopted to approaching both health and development. This includes biological development of the brain and genes, psychological areas including emotions and cognition and social which encompasses perceptions of the self and the self in relation to social settings. The biopsychosocial model differs from the biomedical model, which attributes disease to only biological factors and considers other disciplines such as psychology and sociology not only in treating individuals but also in services and professional's responses to child health (Engel, 1980). This leads to thinking about how development and holistic health and upbringing were addressed in the past.

Development and holistic care

In 1860, it was estimated that 15–20 per cent of infants died before their first birthday. An additional 10 per cent would die before the age of five. By the late nineteenth century, the emerging field of paediatrics advanced in science with the aim to reduce disease and child mortality through an application of science knowledge and intervention (Grant, 1998). The late nineteenth century was a period when psychology, as a discipline, emerged as a separate science, including the study of child development. In 1870s, Darwin published *A Biographical Sketch of an Infant*, from observing and studying his own infant son's behaviour. Emmet Holt also took a scientific approach to child-rearing, specifically advice to mothers with a bid to prevent and improve poor outcomes (Mintz, 2004). This included strict regimes with feeding and sleeping, as well as avoiding unnecessary pampering or indulgency towards the infant (Mintz, 2004). Such rapid changes from the less structured approaches of the early nineteenth century to strictly controlled approaches of the latter part of the century were brought about by societal shifts and responses to the changing socio-economic climate of the time. This included the concerns with child mortality and associated hazards of urban life (Cushman, 1995).

In 1880 there was an increase in trade union membership and industrial action, because of low wages and employment insecurity. Lord Sainsbury's Conservative government appointed a Royal Commissioner in May 1891, to enquire into workplace conditions and relations between their employees and their employers. The Women's Industrial Labour was identified as a key area of study and in giving their own evidence Booth sent his secretary, an economist, Clara Colett, to East London for three months in 1886 to collect data on women's wage earning for his survey. She was to get acquainted with them and their work. She recorded that obtaining information from the women was challenging because she was considered an outsider. However, she did manage to obtain some contributing information for the report. Booth's publication with Collet's investigation, specifically revealed the situation of women at work in London's East. Included were statistics, particularly regarding pay, with an additional anecdotal explanation (McDonald, 2003). The study was carried out during an interesting period for women. Collet's presence in the East end intersected with the notorious ripper attacks of the time. Concurrently it was an empowering time for women with the female match workers having won a famous victory through their direct action. Collet mentioned these workers and their newly formed trade union as part of her assessment about match workers, and the prolonged strike in July 1888. With the formation of a union, the largest union composed entirely of women and girls in England, their expertise framed the debate about working mothers and gave voice to working women, including those as mothers previously seldom heard (Bhuller, 2016).

Booth's publication revealed the instability of the household, headed by the male breadwinner, and accompanied with insecure employment, frequent illness and unemployment. Miss Sharples (1906), a sanitary inspector, evaluated that many married women who worked outside their home did not do so from choice but out of necessity (Hobby, 1999). The loss of an infant life was a continuing concern in the mid-nineteenth century. In 1880 infant mortality remained high, particularly for mothers who continued to work in heavy manual labour during pregnancy. Premature death and birth defects were often inevitable, and many infants were sent out to nurse whilst mothers returned to work. Unfortunately, being nursed out was an additional cause for concern and the carers often left their charges in inappropriate places, such as soapboxes, as they carried on with their work at home, probably caring for their own and other children as well (Ross, 1993). Reports about infant care hazards such as unguarded fires were a major cause of death among unattended infants. Furthermore, many infants were drugged with opiates in their milk and food to keep them quiet. Contaminated milk and tins of condensed milk were left open for days with dirty fungus bearing bottles and long feeding tubes being the cause of early deaths. A lack of storage and understanding about contamination was often the continued reason as well as infants weaned too early with bread, water and sugar known as bap or fed the same food as the parents, such as fish and chips.

In England a national move to try and improve infant health was introduced. Mothers who had delivered and cared for children under three years were excluded from factories and workshops. The 1833 Factory Act was followed by further Factory Acts, in 1878, 1891 and 1895, whereby Parliament placed additional limits on the employment of women and children in factories, extending earlier safety regulation. The 1891 Act raised the minimum age for employment in factories to 11 years as well as banning women from work who had given birth within four weeks. This was further extended with the withdrawal of women who were six months pregnant and post six months, hoping breastfeeding and rest could be established. One of the aims was to improve the education of the working class in their 'duties' as a full-time mother and homemaker. Infant lifesaving initiatives were further developed and implemented in the early twentieth century (Hardyment, 2007; McCarthy, 2020).

Municipal authorities sent female health visitors into the slums to teach infant hygiene, and they also opened sterilized milk depots and included restaurants for mothers who opted to breastfeed their infant. Crèches were opened in the factory workplace, but these proved less popular, with societal opinions of breastfeeding considered a private affair. The overall societal message in England was to retain mothers in the home whilst the men received more wages. The concept of maternity leave did not become part of the discourse and the four-week exclusion period nationally stipulated in 1891 did not provide any mothers the right to return to work or receive maternity pay. In 1911 the National Insurance Act allowed women workers to be entitled to the maternity benefits of a one-off £3.00, considerably more than the 30 shillings received by a non-earning wife. It covered the costs of linen, baby documents fees and home help. However, all women who had paid National Insurance lost all their entitlements and benefits relating to sickness and unemployment when they got married (McCarthy, 2020a:39; Ross, 1993).

Margaret Forster's (2003) fictitious character in a *Diary of an Ordinary Woman* explored the power of the micro-narratives in history against the backdrop of societal changes. In this story the impact of the two world wars was the societal landscapes to the story. The central story was about an English woman, working in the health sector and themes about motherhood. The fictitious character presents an authentic discourse about the loss of motherhood and 'alloparenting' (caring for other children). It elicited an understanding to relationships and infant care from a political perspective with the restrictions and lived experiences of the time. The *Diary 49 the Wartime Diaries* of Nella Last was non-fiction and depicted her life story during the Second World War. The Diaries were collated by The Mass Observation and continue to be accessible via the University of Sussex, at The Keep archive (The Keep, 2020; McCarthy, 2020). The Mass Observation

Diaries are an innovative social research organization, founded in 1937 to study the lives of ordinary Britain's. Nella was one of the first 500 to volunteer and contribute to writing, via a diary format, about her working life. She included her daily community life and the wider social landscape. She also included micro-stories about her own life and topics regarding her marriage and troubles she faced during her life.

Further ways of understanding the daily lives of those less heard regarding their holistic care of infants during the latter nineteenth century were death reports from coroner's inquests. Holmes (2014) evaluated domestic practice in the homes of the Victorian urban working class and the often-forgotten homes of the rural labouring class. In pursuing a study of coroner reports she discussed the arrangement of the home and stories of family lives with infants. This was another opportunity to examine family life. Generally, autobiographies of family life in the Victorian working-class home were predominately written by men, with a few by women. Autobiographies may not always offer a representative, cross section of working-class homes and domestic practice. Supplementary records and other evidence can therefore develop a narrative beyond the male voice. Whilst described as emotionally disturbing the examination of fatal household accidents through coroner reports provided an authentic and less gendered perspective into the life of domestic households.

Contemplative case study of care

This is an example of a coroner report to illustrate how the reader could learn more about family life.

In May 1871, an inquest was held on an Ipswich infant who was believed to have suffocated in the parental bed; the infant mother's testimony described the family's bedtime routine:

> I retired to bed on Wednesday night – about 9 o'clock – the [infant] was laying on its side. My husband is a labourer ... I suckled the [infant] for the last time between 3 and 4 yesterday [when my] husband got up and went to his work ... I then fell asleep and awoke about ¼ to 6 o'clock on turning around I found the [infant] dead. (Holmes, 2014:321)

'Laying on' was a frequent cause of death whereby the mother or a main carer had fallen asleep and accidently suffocated the infant (Holmes, 2010). Reports suggested cribs were used and the infant was not always placed in the bed with the mother, but because of crying and the thin walls many parents would then take their infant into bed with them at some stage during the night and then fall asleep. Holmes (2014) also highlighted how practices changed in the home. By drawing on coroner reports, alongside newspaper articles during a period of sixty years, she was able to describe infant care.

The individual case stories of those tragic episodes revealed the way many infants and young children were cared for by the accidents that occurred. Many of those accidents were caused by being left near a fire, scolding or overlaying of an infant.

> On a Saturday afternoon Mrs Dewhurst was in an underground kitchen washing one of her children. Clara was sitting tied to a chair by the side of the fire in the front room upstairs when some clothes that were on the guard in front of the fire became ignited and set fire to a cushion against which the child was leaning. Her head was soon in flames and the mother hearing screams ran to the room and extinguished the flames. Subsequently the child was treated at the hospital daily but died from the effects of burning. (Holmes, 2014:317)
>
> Another story was scalding … some boiling water into a small tub standing on the ground in the yard Charles and his sister were blowing bubbles and stepping backwards. He fell into the water. (320)
>
> On Saturday last William's mother was cooking some cabbages on the fire after laying the child on the hearthrug she took the saucepan off the fire when the handle came off in her hand in the saucepan fell and boiling contents on the child. (Holmes, 2014:322)

Interestingly the absence of accidents in particular rooms recorded in the coroner's records was noted. Parlours or front rooms reaffirmed that certain rooms in Victorian homes were not often accessed, and generally reserved for best occasions. Some fatalities resulted from accidents with artificial lighting, either by candles or by the notorious penny paraffin lamps (Hewitt, 1999). Witnesses to accounts also highlighted the communal space of the bedrooms among the working class, where home helpers would sleep in the same room as the married couple and their infant. These stories according to Holmes (2014) represented the minutiae of lives, how their rooms were organized and lived in and the day-to-day domestic chores carried out.

In developing the notion of activism, Mary Sumner is deemed an appropriate inclusion to reflect on. She drew on her Christian faith in reaching out to a wide community, initially in England and then internationally, recognizing the need for healthy development and environments of infants and children. She was passionate about transforming the home-lives of parish families, by helping the women support each other in raising their children. In her life she had a supportive husband and became a public speaker, inspired by her faith. She spoke passionately and importantly, both to husbands and to wives, about showing respect, appreciation and love (Anderson-Faithful, 2018). In 1885, at a time when it was still unheard of for women to speak to large audiences, her reputation grew and by 1876, she had founded The Union of Mothers. She was invited and given authority to speak by the bishop to a large church congregation. Her speeches and general approach were conveyed as a sense of solidarity and unity. This was specifically towards and between women during difficult times, with the religious connection of reaching out to God. The movement grew further, increasingly with the support of bishops, internationally as well as in England.

Key principles developed and these included:

- That the fortune of a nation begins from the family life in its homes

- That family life is the greatest institution in the world for the formation of the character of children

- That faith is the basis of daily family life

- That the tone of family life depends upon the married life of the parents – and ultimately, that example is stronger than precept (Irvine, 2020).

As the movement grew, Mary Sumner advocated, through religion, the nurturing of healthy environments for young children (Mothers Union, 2020). From 1900 onwards, she and members advocated issues of key importance to families and children. She campaigned to stop young children collecting alcohol from public houses for their families, and for the age of marriage for girls to be raised from 12 to 16 years (Anderson-Faithful, 2018).

Contemplative question

Reflect and think about how organizations continue to support mothers and families.

Today The Union of Mothers continues with faith being put into action to nurture healthy relationships in families and communities and to fight for social justice. What other organizations have supported mothers and their infants in a local area and what is their history?

The power of everyday care stories in understanding history and a life lived

During the late nineteenth century working-class women continued to have little access to medical care, nutritious food and domestic help. They were often left alone caring for children during pregnancy in conditions that often predicted a negative outcome for the mother and her infant. The rationale for discussing The *Maternity Letters*, written by The Women's Guild, was the lack of women's autobiographies, alongside national recognition of pregnant women and the lived experiences of caring for their infants during this period in history (Cohen, 2020).

FIGURE 4.2 Mother and daughter looking at the baby (1905).

The Women's Guild was a socialist consumer-based organization designed to put the community in control. The Women's Guild led during this period was Margaret Llewelyn Davies. It was a group that provided an opportunity for women to become part of a movement alongside their husbands. As a small subgroup of The Co-Operative, the women met together and, although they were not deemed the most desolate in terms of poverty, they were still considered working women. Buying items from The Co-Operative and being part of the organization meant they benefitted not only in material goods but also by meeting regularly and sharing their stories together with other women. As The Women's Guild grew in number it strengthened, becoming a platform for women's rights and community activism. One area of this was the issue surrounding maternity (Tilghman, 2003).

Margaret Llewelyn Davies sought to gather testimonies of The Guild's women's living conditions and in 1910 she asked to submit evidence to the Royal Commission on divorce and matrimonial causes. She gathered opinions and personal experiences, and these were published in the form of *The Maternity Letters*. Subsequently the voices of these women provoked an overwhelming response, from the reduction of the cost of divorce in making it more accessible to the general population, as well as highlighting the sexual physical and emotional abuses The Guild's women had suffered because of the legal and economic inequalities between men and women. Based on their willingness to share their private domestic lives, they received the support of the Guild officials. In listening to their voices, the period between 1910 and 1915 was pursued through an active feminist agenda that advocated divorce reform, maternity benefits, female suffrage and the education of women. In 1914 there was a drive for a state-funded national scheme for maternity care that would benefit the almost 7,000,000 married women who had been excluded from the original bill. The maternity benefit became the women's sole property, rather than their husbands'. The Guild women's effort culminated in 1915 with the publication of *Maternity*, the stories bringing public opinion to the fore. This led to the legal and medical professions communicating with The Women's Guild. The published book *Maternity Letters* targeted reader audiences both within and beyond the Co-Operative movement and at local and national levels. It exposed private experiences of many women to the public and because the experiences incorporated stories about social abuse the impact of *The Maternity Letters* proved an effective way in being able to raise public consciousness and motivate legislators. It also spread the virtues of the Co-Operative movement and gave recognition to them (Cohen, 2020).

The Women's Co-Operative Guild's choice of the letter as a means for lobbying government, as a form of life writing, gave detailed accounts of private perceptions of everyday life to a known audience. The letters also formed a group identity establishment because it facilitated and gathered both qualitative and quantitative evidence about the domestic concerns from a specific population of women. The letters themselves repeatedly expressed the need for freedom and effects of the medical ignorance and incompetent maternity care. The women's complaints as political documents were unsettling because of the prevalence and urgency about their cases as well as it being 'typical' and revealing any number of women could have written the letters. Margaret Llewelyn Davies was aware of both the relevance of autobiography and the effectiveness of letter writing as a form of political strategy in her introduction to maternity. In 1914, prior to placing the national care of maternity scheme before the local government board she thought it would be advisable to obtain information from the members themselves. These were to deliberately include the conditions they had bought their infants into the world. In writing the letter the following questions were asked.

- How many children have you had?

- How soon after each other were they born?

- Did any die under five years old and if so what age and from what cause?

- Were any stillborn and, if so, how many?

- Have you had any miscarriages and, if so, how many?

The letters remained in their original form, written by the women, with the only alterations made being in the spelling. Minor punctuation and the omission of a few medical details, all names and places were also excluded to prevent the identification of the women (Davies, 1978a:215).

Written recordings of husbands'/partners' earnings by manual labour covered over 100 different occupations, and their rates of wages varied from 11 shillings to 5 pounds. The letters show how often the nominal wages were reduced by periods of a short time and unemployment. These periods consistently coincided with childbirth (Davies, 1978a:218). Generally, the earnings and conditions of the Co-Operative men were considered above, rather than below, the level of their working class. The Co-Operative movement largely composed of better paid manual workers. Women who had the role as a branch secretary lived in better conditions than the average working woman and although the women in the Guild were working class, they were not considered to be living in absolute poverty, in comparison to other members of society. However, if the conditions of their lives described in the letters were not from the poorest then it highlighted how extreme suffering could be surrounding relative poverty, where wages were less and employment more precarious. The women themselves reflected on their situation and compared it to those less fortunate, including it in their narrative, within the letters. The reader gets a glimpse of their lives, and records of 400 lives were received to the Guild. The book *Maternity Letters* published 160 letters, representative of the 400 (Davis, 1978a).

Case studies of care: *Maternity Letters*

Some examples

Replies were received from 386 Guild members covering 400 cases, with a few not being members of the Guild. A second letter was then sent out asking for particulars of wages and the occupation of the husbands, and the wages received. These details were recorded at the end of the letter. The published letters represented as far as possible with 160 published. The remainder described similar conditions out of the total number of cases, with at least two out of three indicating conditions of maternity which were not normal and healthy. (Davies, 1978a:198)

Husbands' role in conceiving

Men: my husband's wages were very unsettled never exceeded 30 shillings and was often below. I earned a little all the time by sewing. I did all the housework, washing baking and made all our clothes. But no amount of state help can help the suffering of mothers until men are taught many things in regard to the right use of the organs of reproduction. Until he realises that their wives body belongs to herself and until the marriage relations take a higher sense of morality and bear justice and what I implied not only exists in the lowest rate of society but it's just as prevalent in the higher. So it's men who need to be educated ... suffer comes to the mother and child through the father's ignorance.... an interference pain of body and mind which leaves his mark in many ways on the child marriage laws. (Davies, 1978a:13)

I am afraid I cannot tell you very much because I worked too hard to think about how we lived. When my second baby came, I did not know how I was going to keep it. When the last one came I had to do my own washing and baking before the weekend. Before three weeks I had to go out working, washing and cleaning and so lost my milk and began with the bottle. Twice I worked within two or three days of my confinement. I was a particularly strong woman when I was married. There is not much strength left but thanks be to God I have not lost one. I have two girls and three boys. Everyone is strong and healthy. The firm my husband worked for failed them for the most time. He did not work but I can truly say that for the most part of 25 years 17 shillings per week was the most I received from him. (Davies, 1978a:116)

Personal health

During pregnancy I always looked to my diet and as my husband never got more than 24 shillings I had not much to throw away on luxuries. I had plain food such as oatmeal, bacon meat, plenty of bread and good butter ... I never had a doctor all the time I was having children. I've had six, one dead. During my labour I was never bad than for about 3 four hours. I felt I could get out of bed the first day. I never had the doctor, only an old midwife. I am a staunch teetotaller and have been all my life.

I think that drink has a lot to do with some women suffering.. I had one child born without a midwife … we had a lodger who paid us 11 shilling which helps us a bit we were quite comfortably off. (Davies, 1978a:10)

Cleanliness had made rapid strides but never once I remember washing anything but face neck and hands washed. For a whole week we were obliged to lie on clothes. Sheets were stained and the stench … added to this we were commanded to keep the babies under the clothes.. I often wonder how poor little mites managed to live and perhaps they never would have done but for our adoration.. constant admiration for our treasures. (Davies, 1978a:19)

Length of time during pregnancy

I was glad to get up and get about again before I was able because I could not afford to pay a woman to look after me I kept on like that till the 6th child. The little one was expected and then I had all the other little ones to see after.. the oldest one was ten years old … so I was obliged to nurse them … for 20 years I was nursing or expecting babies … no doubt there are others fixed the same way. (Davis, 1978:2)

The consequences was my third child who was not born strong. She had a cough as soon as she was born.. it was a struggle … to have a nurse in for a fortnight. I had to get about to do my housework long before I was fit to do it.. my husband works for co-operative firms. (Davies, 1978a:43)

The narratives revealed the isolation felt by women who had been confined to the home with little cultural input or any leisure time. The women assumed a subservient position regarding discriminatory customs and laws. The publication of the guild's women's life experiences circulated and therefore provided critical information about the ideological frames and normative constraints by working-class women. This was specifically on the topic of reproduction and the economic disadvantages of infant care and support.

Contemplative questions

The previous extracts would be worth reading a few times to gain a sense of the mothers' lived and experienced parenthood. They also provide opportunities for further discussions about motherhood and how they resonate with today.

In reading these extracts what are the differences in care of infants today? Can we resonate with these stories?

What can we learn about the power of voice and lobbying for change in the unity of togetherness?

Connections with contemporary practice

In linking development to holistic care in the twentieth and twenty-first centuries neurobiological research has positioned child development at the heart of translational research, integrating existing new knowledge from a range of present theory, providing new understanding and implications for practice to be considered. Translational research has provided evidence about the interaction between experience and the developing brain. Within neurobiological research and development, it is important to recognize the shift in conceptual thinking from nature versus nurture to nature **with** nurture, highlighting how the environment is centrally linked to the developing brain (Dawson and Fischer, 1994). This consideration reminds us about the importance of relationships and care, even with those infants born into compromising circumstances. It is a reminder about how much we know today through technology and research but concurrently, aware that the stories we read are not so different from the voices we hear today. The power and agency of voice and stories told have the potential to drive grassroots changes and therefore a valuable contribution in advocating change for infants.

Conclusion: A personal note

This chapter resonates both with mothers today and those working professionally with mothers, fathers and carers. The reading of voices was an important aspect I considered helpful to understanding infant care. Although we cannot hear the infants' first-hand perspectives, through the parental voices presented and the way development was considered we gain a sense of their lives and their environmental experiences. It is a reminder of the impact poverty has on families and the challenges faced in those early years when birthing and caring for an infant, whist keeping house and employment sustained. In 2020 the pandemic has resulted in the remerging of new mothers feeling isolated, challenged in seeking professional support and vulnerability in losing jobs, and access to resources previously relied on. In appreciating the power and contribution of voice in many forms, it gives a sense of hope and how the future can be reshaped to support families.

CHAPTER FIVE

The Professionalization of infant care

Introduction and context

Early modern midwifery has been the focus of much research and debate. This chapter provides a glimpse into how caring for infants has evolved into a profession, both in health and in early education and care. It focuses on the developing role of the midwife in supporting families. It is intended to introduce the historical transitions to the role of midwifery supporting families and the implications of infant care rather than extensively documenting the changing professional and political tensions of the role. Maternity nurses and early years practitioners in caring for infants are then introduced. The literature available in recent history in terms of childcare advice concludes the chapter.

> Birth is not only about making babies. Birth is about making mothers-strong, competent, capable mothers who trust themselves and know their inner strength. (Rothman, 2021)

Choices of childbirth

In the seventeenth century most women were confined at home during their labour, with help from untrained midwives. Until the early twentieth century in England, birth predominantly took place in domestic spaces at home. There were attempts to bring birth into hospitals during the Victorian period, promoted by pioneers such as Florence Nightingale, who opened a lying-in hospital. However, many of these clinical spaces were short-lived, often closed due to infection within the wards. Women generally preferred a home delivery, the familiar and in some respects safer space (Andrews, 1909). Hospitals during this period were not considered a well-being centre, and whilst admission was accepted in caring for sick, birthing was thought to be generally safer at home. Hospitals were places sought only by the very poor and the desperate (Leap and Hunter, 2013). However, childbirth continued to increasingly occur in health institutions with hospitals supporting high-risk pregnancies and then all pregnancies in the twentieth century. In 1927, hospital confinement was 15 per cent (Oakley, 1981a). During the Second World War period and after, displacement of families in England meant that for many women they no longer had homes to give birth in and therefore were increasingly confined to institutions. The development of medication and antibiotics also meant postnatal fever became less of a threat and therefore hospital wards were considered safer. In the 1950s, the debate shifted to encompass not just the physical setting of birth, home or hospital, but an increased discourse about risk and safety, the use of technology and the management of healthcare under the National Health Service (Leap and Hunter, 2013). General opinion among obstetricians was the physical safety of mother and infant as being the primary goal of maternity services. They argued this was achieved in hospitals with trained obstetricians supervising labour and birth. In 1959 the official view was that 70 per cent of women should have their infants in a hospital setting. By 1960 35 per cent of births took place at home. In 1970, policy stated that there should be enough provision for all women to have a hospital birth. Therefore in 1974 hospital births had increased to 96 per cent and 99 per cent in 1975 of first-born infants in hospitals. Although there were variations normally the mother and new-born would stay for six to ten days in hospital (Oakley, 1981a). The option of a hospital birth and the care received was not always positive. Oakley (1981a) evaluated mothers' narratives of their experiences, transitioning to parenthood as a first-time mother.

Contemplative case study 1: Voices of mothers experiencing hospital care in the twentieth century

Mothers' experience in the 1970s:

> It feels like a cattle market at a production line ... There was the voice of authority, like a parrot, no tone in their voice they just say their bit ... don't hear, don't have time to get involved with people. (Oakley, 1981a:281)

A computer and being computerised terribly, impersonal mothers perception of medical. (Oakley, 1981a:282)

They kept saying relax, but quite rough, mechanical, embarrassed about being examined ... male dominated. (Oakley, 1981a:283)

Connections with contemporary practice

In the latter twentieth century, many doctors deemed hospital birth safer than home birth, and policymakers supported this move (Norman, 2019). Women desired hospital birth for a variety of reasons. Often it was due to accessing pain relief, which they may not have received at home. Furthermore, women increasingly demanded access to the technology which was becoming available. Epidural anaesthesia, induction of labour and foetal monitoring were obtainable only in a hospital setting. Foetal ultrasounds were available since the 1950s and were initially used for clinical purposes in 1956. Glasgow accessed it from 1950 and Bristol from the 1970s for clinical practice and then routine use (Gordon, 2019). By the end of the twentieth century ultrasounds were available in maternity clinics as part of the observations process (Gordon, 2019). From the mid-1990s government policy has swung back in favour of encouraging home birth for at least some groups of women, but the impact on practice has been minimal. Today in 2021 the stay in hospital is much shorter, especially for low-risk pregnancies. Whilst hospital births remain high there is also an increasing desire by mothers deemed low risk to opt for home births (McIntosh, 2017).

The rationale of professional help

Until the early nineteenth century childbirth was very much a female affair of proceedings with specialized male midwives' doctors called upon only in emergency and difficult births. Female midwives tended to deliver a live infant, whereas a doctor was generally only called to deliver an infant who had little chance of survival, subsequently replaced by male-trained midwives. Husbands tended to be nearby at home, but not physically present during the delivery. Several friends were also available. Additionally, a variety of birthing positions were employed, and birthing stools used, but from the early eighteenth century it was increasingly common to have a bed delivery. A room was prepared for lying in, and this included no light or air after birth with two weeks in bed and then two weeks in the house recommended (Coles, 2015; Roberts, 1995a).

Contemplative case study: Connections from the past

Preparing for birth

In her 1896 book, *Preparation for Motherhood*, author Elizabeth Scovil advised on the proper hairstyle for the delivery room. This was not as shallow as it sounded and certainly women today continue to prepare themselves physically in preparation for a potentially long labour. Many Victorian women had very long hair and if it wasn't braided during their confinement, it could become extremely knotted that the strands of hair would have to be unravelled with a needle.

As Scovil explains: 'Hair forty inches long that had been untouched by comb or brush for three weeks, had been disentangled, but it is a task that equals one of the labours of Hercules.' To prevent this Scovil advised that during the first signs of labour, the expectant mother's hair should be styled into braids. 'The hair should be parted in the middle at the back, firmly braided in two tails and tied so it will not come unloosed. It is then no great matter if it cannot be brushed or combed for several days. It will be found smooth and untangled when it is unplaited' (Matthews, 2016:1).

This is a gentle reminder that the past often mirrors our present and Scovil's description could have been about an expectant mother today. Certainly, from a personal perspective remembering the ritual of washing and tying long hair back in preparation for the labour was something familiar. As a micro story it reveals the everyday lives of personal care and organization for the impending time in labour.

The close association between birth, death and the midwife's role

In the eighteenth century there was little success of delivering an obstructed infant alive and many instruments were used to remove a dead infant, with the primary focus of saving the mother.

Although midwives were criticized by Locke (1690) for meddling unnecessarily in the birthing process, for many the reliance on a midwife was part of the birthing process. Midwives had the confidence and experience adequate for birth, unless there was an obstruction or complication (Heywood, 2017).

In the 1830s childbirth continued to be both painful and dangerous. The discovery of anaesthetics did not occur until 1830 alongside the development of surgical techniques. Prior to this pain management occurred in numerous forms. The only pain relief available was opium, usually sold as a sleeping drink, as laudanum, although typically it was rarely used. It was widely believed that women were destined to suffer during childbirth, as the Bible had decreed. However, it was a misconception that the birth of an infant was not welcome. Pollock (1987) suggested they were indeed welcomed, as a diary entry in 1709 recorded. The diary described the pain felt in her abdomen and the fear of miscarrying. She therefore prepared by resting at home and recovering, with a successful delivery two weeks later (Pollock, 1987).

However, pregnant women and their husbands approached each birth with trepidation. Many women routinely prepared themselves for death and the terms they used to describe 'lying-in' afterwards reflected this (Kunzel, 1993). As well as the assistance of family and friends there were also women who practised childbirth. These were known as handywomen, midwives. Although there was no formal training, most women were experienced midwives who had given birth to several children themselves. Doctors were relied on when births were prolonged and feared that the mother might die, although there are stories of doctors themselves cross-infecting during childbirth, not adhering to self-hygiene practices, having come straight from supporting previous patients (Ross, 1993). The main dangers for women in childbirth were prolonged birth, excessive bleeding and infection. Prolonged and challenging births of labour were generally because the infants were in the breech (feet-first position), or transverse (sideways) position. There were dangerous attempts made to turn infants, but this was rarely successful. In extreme cases, after two or more days in labour a doctor may use instruments to remove the infant (Leap and Hunter, 2013).

During the nineteenth century a midwife or doctor could rarely stop a post-birth haemorrhage and many women bled to death. Alongside infection these were the main causes of death during childbirth. Childbed fever generally set in two or three days after birth, but once established had an almost inevitable outcome. The actual cause of death tended to be blood poisoning or septicaemia, generally between a week and ten days after delivery (Anderson, 2013).

Connections with contemporary practice

Full term is 40 weeks; however, the earliest a baby can survive is about 22 weeks gestation. The age of viability is 24 weeks. At 22 weeks, there's a 0–10 per cent chance of survival; at 24 weeks the survival rate is 40–70 per cent. Technology and professional care and support assume improved life outcomes for both infant and mother. However, even though modern medicine has saved infants a few weeks old, many families continue to face a reality of children with complex needs. Gordon (2019) discussed her personal journey, presenting her dilemmas of prenatal screening, laser surgery and how modern-day foetal medics reflect on their own roles (Gordon, 2019:1).

It reminds us that historical stories about mortality, professionals, technology, instruments and care have not diminished with time but rather shifted in the discourses about pregnancy and childbirth. Although arguably less, for those women deemed as high-risk pregnancies, each birth continues to be approached with trepidation paralleled with an empowering time for women.

The forms of professional help: The local community midwife

Regarding difficult births medical practitioners, alongside medical books, tended to draw on the work of *Culpeper's Directory* (1616–54) for midwives. This was a guide for women and translations of the anatomy. This book perceived health as a state of personal balance, with individuals maintaining their own bodies. Many still embraced the humoral models of Aristotle and Galen, with each organ and structure of the body constructed with a purpose of natural qualities and faculties (Culpepper, 1654; William, 1612).

During the Middle Ages the midwife was often blamed for stillbirths, birth defects and the mother's death during birth. She would then be executed due to witchcraft accusations. The male midwife/male doctor was often far less experienced using a limited understanding of anatomy and not using traditional healing practices and herbs. However, he was often called in during difficult births as he would not be accused of witchcraft. Midwifery was one of the many traditions and healing practices of wise women and healers that were once revered and celebrated, then eradicated by the church in favour of men intervening into what was considered women's business (Ehrenreich, 2010).

Jane Sharp (b. 1641) was an English midwife. Her work *The Midwives Book: Or the Whole Art of Midwifery Discovered* was published in 1671. The subject matter was one of the first written and produced by an Englishwoman. No one knows who Jane Sharpe was but as the author of the well-known published midwife book it can be concluded that she was probably a British individual held in esteem about knowing the process of birth. She had access to the private female space of the birthing chamber, the private spaces of women and had a crucial role in the male-dominated church and courts. It was believed she participated in baptism ceremonies and was an expert witness in trials regarding accusations about sexual relations and infants (Hobby, 1999).

Throughout history midwives were often associated as witches, thought to have indulged in witchcraft. They were often called as a witness in trials asked to examine bodies of the accused (Sheridan, 2021). Midwives and handywomen were frequently healers, although often misinterpreted as ignorant. Their male successes were often considered more professional because of their knowledge and use of surgical equipment and skill delivering infants. The reality was birth could be financially rewarding, in delivering live infants. Instruments used such as forceps were a good example of this. The invention of obstetrics forceps in the seventeenth century represented a critically important technical advance in the management of childbirth. However, whilst obstetric forceps were invented in the seventeenth century, they were not widely used during childbirth until the early eighteenth century. The forceps' design was undisclosed and bound up with five generations of the Chamberlen family. The Chamberlens made this obstetric tool a secret for two reasons. The first being that there was opposition at the time within the medical and surgical establishments of using this type of tool during childbirth. It was considered meddling in midwifery; with the concern it could cause undue harm to the mother. A second reason was the financial gain to being the only professionals who could successfully deliver an infant in circumstances deemed problematic (Drife, 2002; Dunn, 1999).

Therefore, deception became an aspect of delivery.

According to Graham (1950) the Chamberlens were said to have arrived at the house of the woman to be delivered in a special carriage. They were accompanied by a huge wooden box adorned with gilded carvings. It always took two of them to carry the box and everyone was led to believe that it contained some massive and highly complicated machine. The labouring woman was blindfold lest she should see the 'secret'. Only the Chamberlens were allowed in the locked lying-in room, from which the terrified relatives heard peculiar noises, ringing bells, and other sinister sounds as the 'secret' went to work (Dunn, 1999:233).

Medical practitioners with experience made a good living from the antenatal care through to childbirth and continued to advise during the early months of the infant's birth. Jane Sharpe paid a substantial £2.00 to obtain a bishop's licence practice. It was illegal to practise without a licence, and this was received after references from medical practitioners, church ministers and clients. Therefore, she had to be practicing before as a deputy midwife for several years. This meant she must have had a flawless character and held in high esteem. Unfortunately, not all midwives met this impeccable criterion. Occasionally widows managed to obtain a licence to gain financial independence and licenced Quaker midwives were active between 1676 and 1718, but there was no figure of how many practised as an unlicensed midwife (Hobby, 1999).

Many women were classed as helpers at birth but also termed gossips. They were often special female family friends and neighbours, chosen by expectant mothers (Leap and Hunter, 2013). Untrained midwives' expertise was generally someone known to them, so many expectant women preferred the care of unqualified midwives for many years. In the passing of the 1902 Midwives Act, unqualified midwives were cheaper generally and retained their friendlier and less likely to tell you what to do persona and being less invasive in the home than by the professionals who visited. Refusal of professional's help remained evident up to the mid-twentieth century (Roberts, 1995a).

Professionalizing the midwife

From 1800 to 1950, maternal mortality was the yardstick for assessing maternity services and it was carefully examined by obstetricians. There were certain problems in defining maternal death including the association of spontaneous abortions, the initial time frame of pregnancy and how long after delivery was the postpartum period. Until the twentieth century this was one month, and from there six weeks, with maternal deaths up to one year still being observed in England. The specific numbers of women dying in childbirth were challenging because there was no national counting of deaths. Until the Registration of Deaths Act of 1837, bills of mortality or parish registers were relied on in recording the statistics (Chamberlain, 2006).

In the early twentieth century untrained local women were likely to be older, respected community members, supporting the health of the sick,

FIGURE 5.1 In training.

the dying or childbirth. County doctors also valued a handy women or midwife to help and train with. The help meant the doctor had more time to deal with complex births. Middle-class women who wanted to professionalize their own contribution to childbirth spearheaded the regulation of training and practice. This formed the Midwives Institute in 1881 using political connections with social reformers and medical professions. The first Midwives Act 1902 was established. The reform meant working-class habits and values drove out the handywoman. A new profession emerged, and the Central Midwives Board (SMB) resulted in restrictions to practise and the introduction of requirements with powerful supervisory operators and disciplinary systems. Ultimately this made it financially impossible for working-class midwives to continue to practise in the long term (Leap and Hunter, 2013). The process for the unqualified midwife was to enrol on the register of qualified midwives to practise for at least one year. They had to have proof of good character with a reference from a clergyman. These midwives were known as bona fides, accepted by authority as stop gaps. Whilst inequality of gender between male and female midwives practising appeared to be reducing, class inequalities were widening. Midwives had to attend higher education, pay fees and pass an exam in Latin. Realistically only those with an education would be able to achieve this. By 1930 only a few handy women were confirmed to practise, with the last bona fide midwife noted as being in 1947 (Coles, 2015; Leap and Hunter, 2013).

Contemplative case studies

These two case studies highlight the challenges from both perspectives and how the community and medical profession viewed the transitions in professionalizing midwives. They provide a useful discussion point of differing positions.

Voice 1: The untrained midwife

Mrs Layton: memories of 70 years

I acted as a maternity nurse and the doctors were satisfied so I was advised to go for midwifery. Feasibly the cheapest training was from £30 to £50, away from home for three months. Unfortunately my husband's health needed care and weekly earnings so it was hard to save.

I was given books and I saw 100 cases a year with doctors doing so little for their fees or cases. I was assumed to be okay do it with low risk deliveries and then they would assist if necessary.

I saved a small amount of money for training but had to be signed by a doctor and he refused because I could not be spared for three months and now knew more anyway than the training could offer ... I therefore gave up the idea ... Ultimately to become a midwife ... but probably wouldn't have if known The Midwives Act was coming along.

Doctors were trained and when I did the 2 hour examination I failed .... always nervous about answering questions ... When midwives became law I was recommended for a certificate as a bona fide midwife. I never let anyone see my certificate. (Llewellyn Davis, 2012:49–51)

Voice 2: The newly trained midwife

Mary, W. grew up in a Yorkshire mining town, experienced resistance to change when she returned as a qualified midwife in the 1930s.

The image of the midwife was of a mature motherly old lady and I didn't get on at all well to begin with. I remember having quite a battle with one of my old aunts. ... she came and watched me bath the baby and she said I like flannels on bairns ... I said well I do occasionally but there's no need for

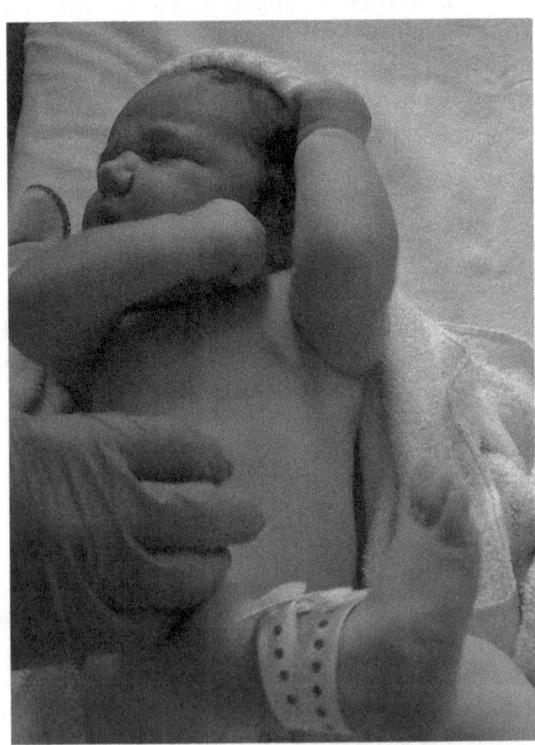

FIGURE 5.2 Infant being examined by a midwife.

it. My new ideas took a lot of getting used to with these people and it was quite a fight with the grandmothers. They had very peculiar old remedies ... putting the babies in bed with them, that was another thing you had to fight. They sometimes had a cradle that was passed down through the family, some would use a drawer or something to put the baby in it if they didn't have a cot, but then again, you'd usually go and find the baby in bed with its mother. I was 25 and practiced in hospital during midwifery training but they thought that experience meant more than training and I was a lass. (Leap and Hunter, 2013:32–3)

Shared infant care

Once the infant was born the midwife was replaced with other forms of infant care within the family home. For many infants born into upper class and aspiring middle classes a live-in nanny was and still is a popular choice for infant family care during the early years. The training and care varied depending on the type of nanny employed and similar to the midwife role, the expectations by the family also varied.

However, the training and expectations have changed in recent times, with a generalized portrait of a nanny from the nineteenth until the mid-twentieth centuries described in the following way

- An unmarried woman, the same class as the wet nurse.

- No formalized training before 1920s and some females entered the profession as young as 12 years under a more experienced nursery nanny.

- Uniform was worn, and the routine was that the nanny would be responsible for the care, bathing and feeding of the infant. They would present the infant to the parents at scheduled times, in their 'best' clothes.

- One nanny reported she could not understand why the parents had babies as there was such little interest in them.

- After five years of age of the children, the nanny was often replaced by governor (Hardyment, 2007:117–119).

Burnett (1984) published autobiographies seeking to identify life stories from libraries, record offices and private memoirs from families. The criteria in their study were that the writers were working class at least for part of their lives, they wrote in English and they had lived in the UK. These autobiographies ranged from 1790 to 1945.

One entry was of a housemaid. She started by talking about herself and going out to work in 1905. She was 14 years and one of eight children.

In her role as a nurse housemaid, she looked after three families in total. One of her families had three children – a baby girl and two boys – and she received two shillings a week.

In the morning I did the housework, and in the afternoon, I took the children out, in the evening I looked after them and put them to bed.

My employers didn't have much money themselves. He was a clerk, but they liked the idea of having a house maid and made me buy and wear a cap, collar, cuffs and an apron. Then the mistress took me to have a photograph taken with the children grouped around me. Perhaps someone still has that photo of themselves … showing the nanny with her charges. I was nearly 17 years, then I left to better myself. (Burnett, 1984b:216)

Nannies were also popular and the well-known story of John Bowlby (1907–90) regarding his nanny, Mini provided an insight into some of his developing theory about attachment. John Bowlby saw his parents once a day and was in the sole charge of Mini until he was two years old. He claimed he never recovered the loss of her mothering approach and love. The separation anxiety he experienced when she left the family home, replaced by another employee, stayed with him into adulthood. Winston Churchill, among other eminent individuals, also had wet nurses, and, whilst seldom discussed, evidence confirms they were present at their nannies' funerals, highlighting their lifelong connections to them. The deep rooted psychological, maternal relationships that existed between nannies and their charges impacted on how and who infants were cared by, through to adulthood (Coles, 2015).

Training in childcare

In 1909 it became evident there was a need for training in infant care and predominately the blame was targeted at poor mothering rather than societal issues. As a national drive to support infant care attention was given to training institutions.

Jane Read (2019) highlighted two training centres, providing an analysis about the complexities of combining education and care. Norland was founded 1892 and was the first education establishment to offer childcare training. Emily Ward initiated the establishment, and it was structured around nurturing and caring. Emily Ward's handwritten manual diary was found 125 years later. It included descriptions of supplying the public with ladies as trained nurses for children. However, what was significant was the social status regarding this type of nanny. They were considered an educated equal, and their position was distinct from the servant model of the time. The nursery nurses worked with, not instead of, the mother (Stokes, 1992). Wellgarth Nursery Training College was similar, although trained girls were from artisan classes rather than the upper classes who wanted to work with infants and children. Prior to the opening of nursery nurse colleges such as Wellgarth, women worked as unqualified child-minders and in crèches. The Women's Industrial Council was formed in 1894 with the intention to open a nursery training school. This was to give girls seeking childcare work an improved understanding about infant and young children's physical needs with some knowledge of child development. It also provided a crèche for working mothers (Read, 2019).

Professional help and advice books

Good mothering, or good enough as Winnicott describes in the 1960s, was an invention of modernization of traditional societal views about the development and happiness of infants younger than two.

Literature in the form of advice manuals was another form of childcare offered to mothers. Prior to the twentieth century childcare advice was also written by clergymen, with morality and development of character being central, targeting parishes to read them and follow their godly advice. 'Character, a kind of moral toughness and integrity, could be "strengthened" through hard work, self-sacrifice, religious observance, and adherence to strict moral laws' (Cushman, 1995:64). Indeed, infant care manuals suggested practices such as giving infants cold baths to toughen them for their life ahead (Grant, 1998).

The first advice manuals included William Cadogan's 1749 *Essay on Nursing* and William Buchan's 1804 *Advice to Mothers*. Books like these were the beginning of the medicalization of motherhood. For physicians in the seventeenth and eighteenth centuries, advice was about physical care and the socialization of children's feeding, toilet training, crying, sleeping, anger and independence implied issues of character as outlined in Cadogan's (1749) publication. Printed advice literature was intended to support parents in the rearing of their infants. This signalled a historical transition regarding the social distribution of knowledge through print across society regarding how infant care is valued. In many cultures, across space and time, child-rearing advice was through oral guidance, with grandparents and other members of the extended family living with or near parents, available to share opinions and participate in the rearing of children. Initially the printed material was written by physicians and then by ministers, with matters of morality and character included at the forefront. The appearance and development of the printed genre in the seventeenth century suggested there was an increased physical mobility of families, who might have moved away from their extended family to urban communities, therefore receiving less oral advice and seeking it in print form. Simultaneously, the rise of certain professions with legitimized expertise resulted in many parents distrusting their own instincts and seeking professional advice about child-rearing (Cunningham, 2017).

The Enlightenment emphasized a reconceptualization of childhood as a distinct and separate stage in life, and therefore advice was offered regarding nurturance and guidance (Hardyment, 2007). Jean Jacques Rousseau, amongst others, viewed the infant as an innocent creature of nature, a contrary view to the current thinking of the time. This was the inherently sinful infant, being a battle of wills between their parents. Physical punishment of young children was also a way of shaping their behaviour and character and this had deep religious roots and meanings. It was not until the middle of the nineteenth century that mainstream Protestant ministers urged parents to gently mould their young children towards good and that they were not innately sinful. Advice to parents softened from the eighteenth century, with a more child-centred approach adopted. Experts writing in the eighteenth century tended to view the family as a microcosm of society, with human interactive relationships being nurtured and understood in the family. From the mid-eighteenth century, scientific psychology provided several theories of child development aimed at linking childhood experiences with behaviour and thinking. The psychology of the child after the late nineteenth century was significant with the publication of Charles Darwin's (1872) *The Origin of Species*. Evolutionary psychology acknowledged instincts and unconscious drives as features to be aligned with rearing infants and therefore advice was about guiding behaviour with positive activities However, with industrialization and urbanization of family life, advice manual writers emphasized self-control and self-discipline. Writers advised against parents' expressions of anger, and Victorians in the nineteenth century viewed the ideal home as, an aspirational sanctuary space. Amongst the public activities was the creation of maternal organizations, usually associated with churches. From these organizations came the publications of new forms of literature such as monthly leaflets and magazines aimed at sharing information between mothers (Hardyment, 2007).

Contemplative question: A mother's voice in response to an infant caring approach

What are our thoughts about the following two approaches now and why were and are childcare advice books so popular?

Consider the following example sand discuss your thoughts in relation to some of the themes discussed so far within the chapter.

Voice 1

There was no kissing and I was to leave my baby at the back of the garden to sleep, I didn't want a screaming baby, one idea of child rearing was that it was wrong to want to love my baby, but this regime was very much against my desires as a mother. (anon)

Voice 2

In 1944 I would put my baby in a pram and leave him as advocated at the time. Unfortunately, at 18 months he got ill as a result and was admitted to hospital. I was not allowed into the ward to see him or cuddle him. He was not even allowed a cuddle cloth or toy from home. (anon)

Arnold Gesell's (1943) enormously popular childcare book *Infant and Child Care in the Culture of Today* diversified from a behavioural approach. He popularized a developmental approach that emphasized the growth of the unique individual, aimed at a more democratic family and democratic society. The child-centred approach provided a more relaxed approach to feeding, toilet training and independence training (Grant, 1998). This paved the way to *The Commonsense Book of Baby and Child Care*, by Benjamin Spock (1945), which became a best-seller during the twentieth century. Mothers in latter twentieth century heavily relied on Spock's advice and appreciated his friendly, reassuring tone. Spock stressed parents should trust their own capabilities and have confidence in their instincts (Grant, 1998; Stearns, 2003). Nevertheless, his book remained filled with advice about infant schedules, delaying responses to crying. He also advocated to not overindulge the infant, extending previous advice offered by other authors. In the 1950s, the return to the reliance on expert advice intensified as families moved geographically and philosophically away from existing extended family networks. However, child-rearing advice from Spock remained a helpful guide and valuable to mothers, followed throughout the latter part of the twentieth century (Grant, 1998; Stearns, 2003).

Connections with contemporary care practices

Whilst many popular parenting books such as by Gina Ford and Dr Green are increasingly popular with their regimes, physician William Sears and his wife, Martha Sears, a nurse, were considered much more aligned to duplicating Dr Spock's wide influence. They published predominately in the 1990s and early 2000s. The Sears emphasized the earliest period

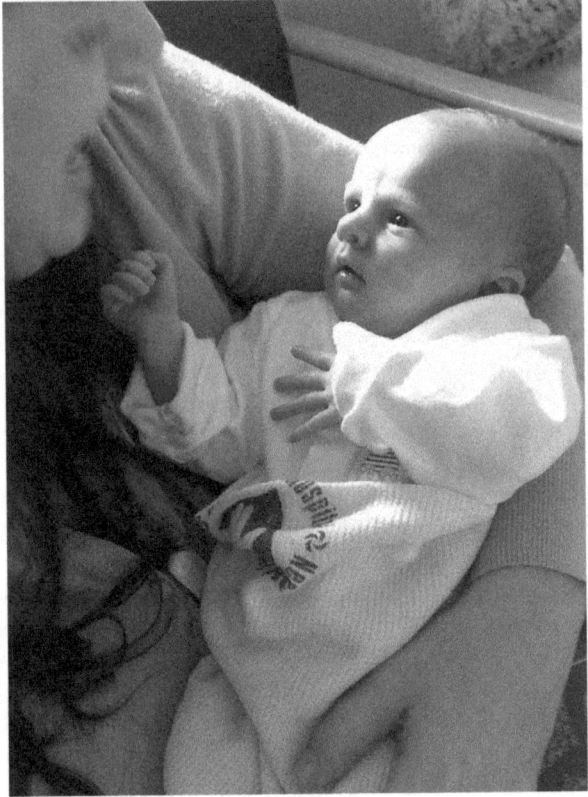

FIGURE 5.3 Creating bonds.

of an infant life as being the most fundamental. Recent studies of early brain development have reinforced this trend. At the centre of their advice is attachment parenting, relating to Bowlby's theories of attachment. It supported breastfeeding for as long as both mother and infant desired and encouraged a prompt response to infant's cries. Co-sleeping and carrying the infant in a sling were encouraged, with the view that parents should be encouraged to maintain sensitivity and care, trusting their own responses to their infant needs.

Connections with contemporary practice

Today popular parenting books can be categorized into three types: infant-led (that promote responding to infant needs), ambivalent (suggesting the parent is the expert who knows best for their infant) and parent-led (promoting parent-led establishment of routine to shape infant behaviour around sleep, feeding and activity). A significant proportion of these books is dedicated to a parent-led approach, proposing routines and schedules for young infant sleep, care and parental engagement (Hardyment, 2007). However, despite their following, the empirical evidence base for these books is weak.

Harries and Brown's (2017) findings showed less than a quarter of mothers reported that they followed the advice in the books or would use them again with their next infant.

Contemplative question

Think about this in relation to what has been discussed in Chapters 1 and 5 regarding parenting advice.

In reflecting on printed advice from the past can you compare whether you think mothers with infants continue to receive less or more conflicting advice about infant care?

Conclusion: A personal note

In exploring midwifery this chapter provided an opportunity to explore how their role transformed from family friend to a profession. In researching the midwifery role from an academic and personal perspective it enabled a deeper understanding to the hesitancy of using both locally untrained members and professional and unfamiliar outsiders. In reviewing this I wanted to include a short extract from both perspectives in hearing their voice and interpretations of their role. It aids an appreciation of the complexity in seeking home help regarding infant care. This led on to further complexities and financial constraints with hiring a nanny and the training of nannies compared to those untrained. Parenting books continue to be popular to gain knowledge in caring for infants. However, many tend to draw on one perspective with the authors at times directing forms of care without consideration of the ways families behave or question the advice given. The books are therefore devoid of the cultural or individual contexts parents have faced about birthing and caring for infants when reading the advice. Therefore, they should be viewed as complimentary alongside other forms of infant care advice offered.

FIGURE 6.0 Infant.

Item No. T03129 Dame Barbara Hepworth 1903–75

Tate Images 2020

PART TWO

The infant beyond the home

CHAPTER SIX

A caring community

Introduction and context

Today we recognize early intervention as essential to reducing the negative impacts of economic disadvantage, increasing social mobility and preventing some of the risks that can threaten a young child's future. For many families there is a recognition that state financial and social support by intervening early is vital before families deemed at risk reach crises. This chapter begins with an examination about how communities from the past supported those deemed at most risk and needing social support and help financially. It discusses the types of services offered within the community, including the workhouse and its admission procedures. This leads to a description of alternative services offered exclusively to mothers with infants, known as The Foundling Hospital. The Foundling Hospital and its relevance to infant care are then discussed with links to contemporary practice. It remains a charity today continuing to inform, providing a valuable example about how social support remains critical to community infant care.

The chapter then concludes with a more recent historical example from the mid-twentieth century illustrating the challenges regarding community care and how actions can influence and inform changes for the future. *Cathy Come Home* provides a popular example to the complexities of family life and community infant care.

It is not all in this bargain that you need become attached to my child or that my child needs to become attached to you. I don't expect or desire anything of the kind. Quite the reverse. When you go away from here you will have concluded what is a mere matter of bargain and sail, hiring and letting and will stay away. The child will cease to remember you; and you will cease, if you please to remember the child. (Dickens, 1844: A Christmas Carol, 28-29)

Poverty and the community

The Poor Relief was the basis to The Old Poor Law of 1601. This became known as the Elizabethan Poor Law and remained in effect for over 200 years. It put all the previous Poor Laws together into one Act, setting up a legal framework to tackle the problem of the poor. It also encouraged the establishment of alms houses. These were places built and supported by private donations that were meant to look after the deserving poor. The parish was the focus of the administration of poor relief, funded by a local property tax known as the poor rates. Those in need were primarily helped by relief handouts, including cash or other means (Slack, 1995a). The 1601 Act seldom mentioned pauper children, except they were put to work or apprenticed. At the end of the seventeenth century larger towns began to obtain their own local Parliamentary Acts, enabling them to manage their own poor reliefs at a town rather than a parish level. Money was raised specifically to finance the running of large workhouse from 1720s. Parishes were able to discourage claims for poor relief by making the workhouse the only available option. The running of the workhouse by private contractors could reduce the cost to a parish by physically relieving its poor and those in need from the local community. Therefore, the opening and operational workhouse became an attractive money-saving proposition in towns, centralizing 'community care' (Berry, 2019). One critical issue for the community was the increasing expense of looking after the poor, with the cost paid for by the middle and upper classes in each town, through their local taxes. There was a suspicion amongst the middle and upper classes that they were paying the poor to be lazy, avoiding work.

After years of complaints, a new Poor Law was introduced in 1834, the Poor Law Amendment Act 1834. The new Poor Law was meant to reduce the cost of looking after the poor and impose a system which would be the same all over the country (Slack, 1995b). Under the new Poor Law, parishes were grouped into unions and each union had to build a workhouse if they did not already have one. Therefore, individuals living in poverty and needing support would receive help it if they were prepared to leave their homes and go to live and work in the workhouse (Higginbotham, 2017).

The Union Workhouse from 1834 had new policies, including strict segregation of male and female, the elderly and the able-bodied. Children and families were separated, and children under seven years of age lived in women wards, operating a type of nursery facility. Provision was often basic, and parents could request a weekly family supervised daily interview with their children. Sunday afternoons were generally the time they could meet (Berry, 2019; Hendrick, 1997). Conditions inside the workhouse were always deliberately harsh, so that only those who desperately needed help would ask for it. The poor were made to wear a uniform, and the diet was a repetitive offer of bland food. There were also strict rules and regulations to be followed. Inmates, male and female, young and old were made to work hard, often doing unpleasant jobs such as picking oakum or breaking stones (Higginbotham, 2017). Children could also find themselves hired out to work in factories or mines.

However, many people welcomed it because they believed it would:

- reduce the cost of looking after the poor,

- take beggars off the streets,

- encourage poor people to work hard to support themselves.

The new Poor Law ensured that the poor were housed in workhouses, clothed and fed. Children who entered the workhouse would receive some formal education through schooling. In return for this care, all workhouse populations would have to work for numerous daily hours. Some members of the community did not view the workhouse as being beneficial for the working classes. Some people, such as Oastler, spoke out against the new Poor Law, calling the workhouses 'Prisons for the Poor'. Individuals from the working class hated and feared the threat of the workhouse, with riots often held regarding its existence (National Archives, nd).

In 1913 the Local Government Board decreed that no healthy child under the age of three should be living in a workhouse after 1915. The workhouse system was abolished in the UK by the same Act on 1 April 1930. However, many workhouses were renamed Public Assistance Institutions and continued under the control of local county councils (Berry, 2019). Whilst the workhouses declined many also changed their premises to hospitals, rather than abruptly closing as suggested. Furthermore, for many years individuals would resist hospital admission, feared by the older generation, because the premises were a reminder of the workhouse regime.

The fear was revealed in Burnett (1984) autobiographies. A grandmother in the early 1900s was old and feeble and considered too unfit to live alone but feared the workhouse. She was living on parish relief, one shilling and sixpence. The relieving officer decided she must be put in the workhouse. The family collectively supported the grandmother rather than allowing her the experience of the workhouse as an elderly woman.

> This upset mother terribly. The workhouse was a horrible place and granny had been such a good mother and worked so hard for many years that it seemed all wrong. My brother seeing my mother upset offered to pay mother 5 shillings a week for the rest of granny's life if mother could have her and look after her. Father was willing. She was 98 years when she died. Harry paid the funeral expenses, so she did not have a

pauper's funeral. Harry himself was only 32 years when he died. (Burnett, 1985a:293)

The fear towards the workhouse seemed to cast a shadow among poor families as they lived their daily lives. This autobiography also highlighted the additional burden of caring for infants alongside elderly relatives.

In 1918 The Save the Children Fund was formed by Eglantyne Jebb, and in 1923 Jebb had drafted the Declaration of the Rights of Children, the first such document to recognize children's rights. This was subsequently adopted by the League of Nations in 1924. Recognizing children had rights grew significantly throughout the twentieth century, until the passing of the UN Convention on the Rights of the Child in 1989, ratified by the UK in 1991 (Mulley, 2019). In 1989 the United Nations Conventions on the Right of the Child (UNCRC), an international human rights treaty, granted all children and young people (aged 17 and under) a comprehensive set of rights, including

- to grow up in a family environment atmosphere of happiness and love and understanding,

- to provide foster care and adoption that supports the continuity of a family upbringing (McNamee, 2016:76).

Life in a workhouse

Contemplative case study: Voice 1

One story recalled from the popular book and television programme, Call the Midwife, was the story of an elderly homeless lady from the 1950s who had a cry like no other sound. She recalls losing her four children to the workhouse. All had died within a short time of entering the workhouse and the story was a desperately sad depiction of life during the early 1900s. It began with the lady being young and married. Her husband worked and they lived modestly. He contracted Tuberculosis. Within a very short space and with very young children, and an infant there was no income apart from the mothers. Unfortunately, due to a severe work accident she could not retain employment. The story described, as a result of loss to income, the selling of furniture and clothes as an attempt to be able to afford to eat. The mother then had to resort to cutting and selling her hair, then teeth to purchase food to survive. It was after this time that she resigned to entering the workhouse, unknown to the children. They were separated on entry and did not see each other again. (Worth, 2005:229–30)

Connections with contemporary infant care and housing

The stories and voices are a reminder of how circumstances can shift so quickly, with the increasing numbers of homeless through varied circumstances. At the Foundling Museum in 2019 a photographic exhibition documented the conditions of London's most disadvantaged infants and children. In partnership with The Childhood Trust, *Bedrooms of London* presented by photographer Wilson focused on the damaging consequences for children, arising from the shortage of social housing in London. Centring on the domestic spaces where children slept, the photographic images, alongside first-hand narratives from families, offered a poignant insight into the lives and experiences of children living in poverty across London. Shown in the context of the Foundling Museum, the exhibition highlighted the situation for some of London's most vulnerable infants and children in contemporary society (Walker, 2018).

Infants in the community

'Foundling' is a historic term applied to children, usually infants, who have been abandoned by their parents. Since Shakespearean days Lords and Mayors took control of hospitals, previously attached to monasteries. The Mission of Christs Hospital was founded in 1552 and housed fatherless children. Over time the practice of leaving foundling infants at hospitals was at first rationed than discouraged altogether because it added a rate-paying burden within parishes (Howell, 2005).

Thomas Coram (1668–1751) returned to London in 1704 after spending time in America, and he was emotionally moved by the visible, desperate poverty he witnessed in London, particularly of infants and young children. As a result of poverty or illegitimacy parents, unable to care for their infants, abandoned them in the streets. After seventeen years of campaigning, Thomas Coram finally received a Royal Charter from King George II in 1739, that enabled him to establish The Foundling Hospital. This hospital was to care for and educate some of London's infant and children. The artist William Hogarth and the composer Handel were eminent supporters who helped establish the hospital, alongside the prominent wives who proved influential to the cause (Hearn, 2020).

Hogarth's paintings depicted the impact of alcohol on infant care, with urban scenes of Gin Lane and Beer Street during the mid-eighteenth century. He portrayed Gin Lane as a scene of murderous and consumptive chaos, infants sick and weak looking, old and shrivelled. Mothers also looked old and worn. Beer Street was a much more favourable illustration, with beer

FIGURE 6.1 Foundling girls at prayer in the Chapel, Sophie Gengembre Anderson (*c.* 1877).

being conceived as good ale. It therefore included a healthier portrayal of mothers and infants and less chaos in the street (Howell, 2005).

The first infants were admitted from 1742, although the plight of caring for the most vulnerable remained, with legislation needed to sustain the operation of The Foundling Hospital, the workhouse and local reform in the community (Shorter, 1976). In 1766 the unhealthy conditions that continued to exist in many London workhouses prompted the passing of Jonas Hanway Act. Hanway was particularly concerned with the expanding

FIGURE 6.2 Gin Lane, William Hogarth (1750–1)

population of Britain. He was elected governor of The Foundling Hospital in 1756 after his substantial donation. With the House of Commons' decision to subsidize The Foundling Hospital, Hanway oversaw the general admission period (1756–60), when infants were admitted. Whilst this attempt proved too costly to continue for long, Hanway was fully invested in the process, involving himself in a variety of concerns around health and daily operations.

Hanway also advocated for policy change, leading to two Acts, both of which would become known as Hanway's Act (Vargo, 2017). The first one,

FIGURE 6.3 Beer Street, William Hogarth (1751)

passed in 1762, required parishes to keep records regarding the children in their care and formed the foundation for later reform work. The second one, passed in 1767, stemmed from Hanway's belief that London was deadly to children who lived in the workhouses. The new policy mandated by the Act relocated infants born in London workhouses to rural environments, placed in baby farms or privately run homes. Whilst the system was later mistreated, the Act saved many lives (Conelln, 2018). The continued interest to infant welfare also came from the wider ramifications of public health movements. Once programmes for public cleansing, drainage and water supply were established, attention focused on infant survival (Holman, 2003; Hendrick, 1997:44). From the end of the eighteenth century the protection and well-being of children was considered the responsibility of the family and society was not expected to intervene with the family. From the beginning of the nineteenth century, the depiction of childhood somewhat changed, and the infant was viewed as precious being, needing to be nationally protected (Bolzman, 2009). The protection of the young child therefore transformed from a private concern to a state concern, within an international platform (Cunningham, 2017).

Connections with contemporary practice: Historical research

The Fallen Women (2015) exhibition at the Foundling Museum provided an opportunity for new research into the hospital's nineteenth-century records which, unlike their eighteenth century counterparts, remained largely unexplored. The archives revealed the hospital's admissions process during Victorian times. Among them were the petitions, which were pre-printed forms a mother had to complete if she wanted The Foundling Hospital to consider her infant for admission. The petitions were the first step in a very thorough investigative process designed to determine both the circumstances behind her infants' birth and the mother's moral character. The petitions were the result of a change in the Hospital's admissions policy in the early nineteenth century. Previously infants were admitted for many reasons, including poverty and the death of parents. As the number of spaces was limited and the request for a place remained high, only illegitimate infants were then accepted, although illegitimacy on its own was not enough. The infants had to be the first and from a previously respectable woman. The mother was therefore defined as a 'fallen' woman, someone who had lost her position in society as a result of sex outside marriage (Kunzel, 1993; Nead, 2015).

Admission to The Foundling Hospital

Initially the process of admission to The Foundling Hospital in the eighteenth century was for the mother and infant to step forward and draw up a ball. If a white ball was selected an infant was admitted taken immediately. The infant would normally be under two months and free from infection. If a black ball was selected this resulted in the mother and infant being turned away. A red ball placed the women in another room, waiting to see whether her turn would come if an infant with a white ball would later be rejected (Cowan, 2021).

In the face of overwhelming increasing demand for limited places, The Foundling Hospital viewed their new admissions policy as a chance to rescue the mother and infant from a life of certain destitution. It was an opportunity of saving the Mother from shame, and of enabling her to return to her proper situation and situation in life with her moral character redeemed (Howell, 2005).

During this period women were often trying to escape the workhouse, where infant mortality was extremely high and in regaining respectability, both mother and infant inevitably had to be parted. It was perceived in society as shameful to be born out of wedlock and resulted in restricted employment opportunities. This view continued all the way through to the twentieth century, and Cowan's biography depicted her own mother's experiences as a foundling child. It provided a powerful narrative about the foundling system during the twentieth century. It also collaborated with the stories regarding the stigma of unmarried mothers and the lasting impact on family relationships and relatives (Cowan, 2021).

As the admission process changed and became more selected in its applications, it included much more paper processing regarding the mother's background circumstances. Detailed personal information was provided, including name and occupation of the father, with information about the last time they had seen him. This was supported with a statement describing the circumstances that led to the woman becoming pregnant. The statements provide an immediate and powerful sense of the situation by women who became pregnant, outside of marriage (Moorhead, 2015; Nead, 2015).

Contemplative case studies of women and their foundlings

These voices provide an insight into the conditions and circumstances of women who accessed the hospital. Harriet Hooper, whose child was accepted in 1865, wrote:

> In April he took me to a house in the New North Road stating that he would introduce me to a friend who had a piano forte [which] would have been of use to me in singing – I found however there was no pianoforte but a bed ... I wished to leave but he prevented me and kept me for some time,

Susannah Jane Keys, who had recently given birth to twins, explained that the father of her children was a lodger at the home of friends.

He had seemed respectable and came to visit her at her father's house, but raped her there. She 'resisted and cried out', but there was no one to hear.

Sarah Farquar, who arrived at the hospital with her child in 1854, was different from many, in that she was a governess and so was able to write her own petition. In a series of letters to the secretary of the hospital, she describes how she was drugged and then raped, and that when she later found she was pregnant, 'My first thought was self-destruction and this I attempted twice' (Moorhead, 2015:1).

According to Nead (2015), the mothers knew what they had to say to get their infant accepted into The Foundling Hospital. They therefore had to manipulate some of their personal stories, so they were perceived as respectable. Therefore, the stories may not have been entirely accurate, although provides 'typical' examples of how their circumstances to becoming pregnant had occurred (Moorhead, 2015).

History of The Foundling Hospital tokens

Separation tokens were left with infants and these included a coin or charms or burdens so they could be identified and reclaimed. This was not a new concept, and there is evidence in Greek history and international myth tales of abandoned and reunited highborn by recognition of tokens. Similarly in the eleventh century Catholic religious orders used tokens (Berry, 2019).

When the Hospital first opened its doors in 1741 mothers were asked to attach some writing, or other distinguishing mark or token, on their infant. Infants were renamed on admission, so the system was introduced in the event of the mother returning to be reunited with her infant. Between the 1740s and 1760s the procedure involved a swatch of fabric being cut from the infant's clothes and then cut in half; one half was attached to the admission paper or 'billet' on which was written the infants unique admission number, whilst the other half was given to the mother (Higginbotham, 2017). Mothers also left an object unique to them, a token as a means of identification. These everyday items range from found objects such as coins, medals and jewellery, to personalized items and, once received, was sealed with the infant's information and token, opened only when a claim was made, and never viewed by the foundlings themselves (Syles, 2010).

Styles (2010) describes the power of these humble objects:

The textiles are both beautiful and poignant, embedded in a rich social history. Each swatch reflects the life of a single infant child. But the textiles also tell us about the clothes their mothers wore, because baby clothes were usually made up from worn-out adult clothing. The fabrics reveal how working women struggled to be fashionable in the 18th century. (Styles, 2010:1)

Contemplative questions

The tokens seemed a poignant and symbolic object identifying the child and connecting them to the birth mother. Discuss the following.

Unfortunately, at some point in the mid-nineteenth century the billets were opened and some of the more interesting tokens were put out on display in the Hospital with good intention as a reminder of the infants. However, no one thought to make a note of which tokens were assigned to the infants and many tokens were unidentifiable (Howell, 2005).

What does this communicate in terms of how infants were valued as individuals living in The Foundling Hospital at the time?

Considering group care what do you think the care would have been like?

As the Foundling Hospital grew and demand increased understanding about childhood shifted, infants were predominately farmed out to wet nurses and foster carers as a way of improving mortality rates. Whilst the families were unregulated aside minimal visits, infants received a range of care, with some receiving a nurturing home, believing their foster parents to be their family. Others were less fortunate and the rationale for wet-nursing and caring until five was predominately an economic decision than a caring one. At five years old the child would then be returned to the hospital and followed a strict regime in preparation for adult life in service of sorts. Children would not be re-connected with their foster families. The hospital eventually closed its doors as a residential institute in 1954. Foundling Voices featured the experiences of seventy-four former pupils whose memories of their childhoods in the first half of the twentieth century have been graphically preserved in audio interviews (Howell, 2005). It provided an insight into their personal experiences and the relationships they formed in the early years cared for by foster families and then within and beyond The Foundling Hospital.

Contemporary state intervention: Learning from the past?

Families living in relative poverty today have a different attitude towards illegitimacy and with state support child abandonment is unusual in England. Although it is considered a serious crime in many countries, including England where it is illegal, there have been exceptions in the form of safe-haven laws. These means infants can be left in designated places such as hospitals or 'baby hatches', which enable parents to safely and anonymously give up the care of their children. This has been criticized by the United Nations. Baby hatches have been reintroduced in Europe and in China where an estimated 10,000 infants and young children are abandoned each year. In 2012 it was reported in a decade that almost 200 baby hatches had been installed across Europe in countries as diverse as Germany, Austria, Switzerland, Poland, Czech Republic and Latvia. The United Nations has spoken out against this practice with a concern it violates the right of the child to be known and cared for by his or her parents (Higginbotham, 2017; Howell, 2005).

In supporting the United Nations Convention on the Right of the Child in England the charity Coram Foundation, built from The Foundling Hospital, continues to retain children at the heart. It offers a range of nursery welfare foster services to support those families in need. It continues to create better chances for young children and their future. This is through numerous services, including:

- voluntary adoption agencies,

- creative therapies to enable vulnerable children to express themselves and make sense of their world,

- helping children to make healthy choices about drugs and alcohol,

- supporting children in the legal system,

- providing supported housing (Coram, 2021).

Although the focus of this chapter has been on The Foundling Hospital, other schemes have also emerged throughout history with religious homes and charities such as Barnardo's offering alternatives for infants. These have been in the form of boarding out or fostering (Higginbotham, 2017). In 1889 Barnardo introduced a pioneering scheme whereby illegitimate infants were boarded out, but near where the mothers were working. Mothers were therefore required to take on domestic service considered a respectable position. On their weekly afternoon off work, they were able to see their infant. The mothers also shared the cost of the boarding out and the employer also received a payment from Barnardo's. If for any reason the mother failed to pay, the agreement was terminated and the infant would return to an institutional home (Higginbotham, 2017).

By the mid-twentieth century institutional care was considered the least preferable option and wherever possible infants and young children were encouraged to retain contact with their relatives and siblings. Interestingly whilst legal adoption had been possible since 1926 it was not something Barnardo had much interest for. It is assumed that he strongly believed his institutional 'homes' were preferable and good preparation for adult life, contributing to society. In 1947 Barnardo became a registered adoption society. In 1948 under the Children Act local authorities were required to set up children's committees and appoint a children's officer to promote welfare of deprived children. This meant that charities such as Barnardo now had to take their place in a national system of childcare and authority of the Home Office Children's Department rather than acting autonomously as they had previously done. National regulation was now at the forefront, with funding and resources monitored (Higginbotham, 2017; Howell, 2005).

In the twentieth century theories of child development were influenced by experiences of the war with family breakdowns, separation and evacuation (Davis, 2012). Whilst we often hear of Donald Winnicott, his wife Clare Winnicott, a social worker, made invaluable contributions post–Second World War, in the 1950s. She recognized the mental health concerns of parents and their infants, alongside the support that was needed. This included more personal and smaller numbers occupying the accommodation facilities for those in need. The use of psychiatric social workers with skill was also available to support the parents. Clare Winnicott acknowledged that whilst many orphanages and homes existed for young children they focused primarily on food and clothes rather than the emotional needs. Institutional childcare therefore lacked something beyond happiness. It was the development of character and qualities of citizenship that failed to be developed and because of the war an increased number of homeless children in England were entering institutional homes. As a scientific lens to child development was developing, the tension between a lack of care and emotion was increasingly observed. Rather than institutions the favourable upbringing was a stable family, with the child accepted and welcomed (Kanter, 2004).

Contemplative case study: Moving to the 1960s and communities of care, Cathy Come Home

Voice 2: Reflections

In depicting family life, images and film can be a powerful medium in exploring social topics. In 1960 a televised play then film provided a fictionalized narrative of a mother's journey trying to keep her young family together, against the backdrop of social inequalities of the time.

Cathy Come Home was a 1966 BBC television play by Sandford, directed by Loach, about homelessness. The play, then produced as a film, tells the story of a young couple, Cathy (played by Carol White) and Reg (Ray Brooks), and their spiral into poverty and homelessness.

At the beginning of the story, Cathy leaves her parents overcrowded rural home and hitchhikes to the city, where she finds work and meets Reg, a well-paid lorry driver. They fall in love, marry, and rent a modern flat in a building that does not allow children. At this stage the introductory scene is typical of a young couple with a positive outlook. Cathy soon becomes pregnant and must stop working, and Reg is injured on the job and becomes unemployed. The loss of income and birth of baby Sean force them to leave their flat, and they are unable to find another affordable place to live that permits children.

They move in with Reg's mother, until tensions develop between her and Cathy in the crowded flat. A kind elderly landlady, Mrs. Alley, rents to them for a while, during which time Cathy has another son, Stevie. Mrs. Alley even allows them to stay when they fall behind on the rent. However, she dies suddenly, and her nephew demands all the back rent, which they are unable to pay. Again, Cathy and Reg aim to find other accommodation but are continually turned down as they can find nothing available that permits children. During this time Cathy gives birth to her third child, a girl they call Marlene. Their new landlord takes them to court, and the judge rules against them. The family are then evicted by the bailiffs. The family then moves to a caravan parked in a camp where several other families are already living in caravans, but the local residents object to the camp and set it on fire, killing several children. Cathy, Reg and their children are forced to illegally squat in a wrecked, abandoned building. They repeatedly try to get housing through the local council. They are not helped because of their many moves and the long list of other people also seeking housing assistance. Cathy and Reg decide to temporarily separate so that Cathy and the children can move into an emergency homeless shelter where husbands are not allowed to stay. Reg leaves the area to seek employment. Cathy's loneliness and frustration result in her becoming negative with the shelter authorities, who are often cold and judgmental towards the women living in the shelter. Cathy's allotted time at the shelter expires while Reg is away, and she and her two remaining children (one having been sent to live with Reg's mother) have nowhere to go. The final scene of the story is when they go to a railway station, where Cathy's children are taken away from her by social services. (Sandford, 1966:1–2)

Connections with contemporary infant care

Today families in the West, and specifically in England, continue to live in poverty and there is continued concern about supporting infants early to improve their life chances. The term 'poverty' needs to be further explored before making assumptions about poverty as a fixed entity. Poverty is relevant to the society and period lived in.

- Poverty: absolute poverty having nothing
- Relative poverty: should be the measurement. UNICEF definition as living in a household in which disposable income when adjusted for family size and composition is less than 50 per cent of the national mean income (McNamee, 2016).

Services to support those living in poverty remain in constant crisis mode, and a lack of supported accommodation and waiting lists for specialist services extend to a year or more. Today support services such as specialist mother and baby units, an inpatient unit service for women with mental health problems during pregnancy on or after birth of their infant, are a valuable service. Figures confirm one in five mothers has ante and postnatal mental health problems, with five out of a hundred with serious mental health problems. The service's main aim is to keep the mother and infant together (Allen, 2016). Specialist staff nurture and support mothers with treatment potentially in late pregnancy until the infant is one year old. In 2011 *The Munro Review* in England emphasized a change in the social work system where it should be child-centred, where voice is valued and so will enable professionals to produce the best judgements surrounding the child. *The Munro Review* (2011) highlighted the importance of a preventative response rather than responsive action. However, specialist mother and baby units remain few with the poverty gap widening and a growing social and political concern. It is well established that homelessness, including those pregnant or with infants, has a negative impact on mental well-being, and people with mental health problems are also more likely to become homeless in the first place.

Conclusion: A personal note

The main purpose of this chapter was to retain the micro stories and voices of families but also to retain the bigger issues of community support and social care. There is, in my opinion, a danger of describing the bigger picture and losing the 'feel' of what families with infant's encounter. I hope this chapter meets both and unravels some of the dilemma's mothers faced. In researching this chapter. Cowan (2021) was a recent source of inspiration, retelling her mother's story as an adult, retelling her life story and her mother's past. It highlighted the tensions of mother–infant relationships and the significance of attachment and challenges of adverse childhood experiences. It therefore raises the need for national investment for families with infants, who have had challenging circumstances early in life.

CHAPTER SEVEN

Communication, love and care

Introduction and context

Communication, love and care discourses, both within the family and professional contexts, are discussed in this chapter. Historically infant care and loving relationships have varied in meaning, from physical closeness and communal living as well as the promotion of bonding and attachment with a primary carer. Key emphasis of understanding infant care will be located and discussed within the twentieth century. Relationships with infants will be examined within the community context, and case studies of hospital and social care will be included to gain an appreciation of both parental and professional understanding towards love and communication. Studies include Rene Spitz (1940s), John Bowlby (1950s) and James and Joyce Robertson's (1960–70s) who focused on infant care within and beyond the home. Communication will then be historically discussed with a focus on Mrs William Parkes (1825) and Domestic Duties. This was a manual of instructions to young married ladies, about managing their households. Mikhail Bakhtin (1981) and Colwyn Trevarthen (2001) conclude the chapter, uniting a contemporary thread between past and present themes about communication and loving relationships.

> Some parents may need help to understand that sharing love and affection with another caregiver is not like sharing an apple or a sandwich where the more people the less there is for each. Love is learned by loving, and we know from the work of Rudolf Schaffer (1977) that by the end of their first year, most infants have formed attachments to several people. Their love for their mother is in no way diminished by this. (Goldschmied and Jackson, 2004:44)

FIGURE 7.1 Family care 1940s.

Tensions of love and affection

Evaluating differing forms of affection throughout history is challenging and at times contradictory. This is primarily because although parents may love or care for their infants, they did not often show affection publicly and rarely documented it. Moreover, affection is often assessed according to the visible touching, holding, verbal expressions and caresses between carer and infant observed. This may have been perceived as minimal with mothers prioritizing her other household and work duties to that of spending time with her infant (Roberts, 1995a). The realities of work, caring for numerous infants and children and social conformity all contributed to a seemingly unaffectionate family relationships throughout history (Hendrick, 1997).

However, relationships were not always so unaffectionate within families and in exploring Burnett's (1984) collections of autobiographies some of the memoirs written by women in the late nineteenth century provided a glimpse regarding close family bonds.

> Six of us slept in one bed, three at the top three at the bottom. My mother always seemed to have a child at her breast and as the second eldest I would often keep her company, sitting on the edge of the bed with her until late at night as she nursed the baby and waited for my father to come home. (Burnett, 1984b:215)

The idea of wanting to keep her mother company late at night provided an intimate snapshot into close loving relationships. It highlights how the mother had potentially nurtured this personal relationship, beyond the recording of satisfying her infant through nursing. In understanding affection Shorter (1976) and Stone (1979) invoked a complex portrait of the early modern family as potentially lacking in affection until the eighteenth century. This was, in part, mirroring Aries's (1962) previous evaluations of the family through his studies of portraits and family reference books. Shorter's (1976) *The Making of a Modern Family* evaluated that mothers did not often view their infant with the same capacities for joy and pain as themselves. Parents generally did not tend to think from their infant's perspective or show empathy to how they were treated or left. He argued that parental attitude was a result of maternal circumstances and community attitudes, priorities being about their work. Infants were therefore a secondary concern and of less significance, continuing through to the eighteenth and nineteenth centuries. Shorter came to these conclusions about mothering and lack of infant care by drawing on written records about the way they were being treated. With the emergence of the cradle infants were often forced to sleep through aggressive swinging and shaking. Other records documented infants being belligerently rocked against loud singing. Another form of practice, highlighting a lack of affection, was the leaving of infants in solitude for hours, swaddled in clothes and neglected. They were also left unguarded by fires or with family-owned animals such as hogs, often roaming freely within the home. Infants were often recorded as filthy, and a lack of care was viewed as important causes of death, parallel to epidemic diseases. This supports the link between the improved understanding about sanitation and then the space to reflect on the condition's infants lived in. For many mothers carrying their infant was not uncommon as they continued their work, although unlike today as an opportunity to bond, when the infants were carried by their mothers they didn't sing or talk to them. There was little evidence to suggest mothers tried to 'wake their senses' or show maternal tenderness towards them (Shorter, 1976:172).

Connections with contemporary practice

Contemplative question

According to Knowles (2020), human bodies are adapted to be a carrying species as part of evolutionary history. However, the human body is considered less fit and strong than that of nomadic ancestors. Therefore, it can be challenging to carry an infant in arms for prolonged periods of time. A robust and safe sling is therefore deemed an appropriate device to enable the continuation to carry an infant. The closeness of carrying has many health benefits such as close contact, touch, regulation of heart and temperature as well as reduction of crying with the motion. This is in stark contrast to Shorter's findings and views about mothers carrying infants.

Would the closeness of being carried by mothers be enough in feeling loved or is interaction necessary when being carried? Do you think by carrying infants there remained a detachment as Shorter describes or a natural closeness as suggested by Knowles?

Modern-day historians from the mid-twentieth century were argued to have relied primarily on sources of the past by ministers, physicians and other moral pundits. They then often evaluated their findings from male sources. These sources generally believed infant mortality was caused by maternal unlovingness or actual neglect. Therefore, the types of evidence used to evaluate the love between infants and their mothers become important when making assumptions about infant care and parental loving relationships. Pollock (1983) provided an alternative perspective, using diaries and personal notes written by women. Furthermore, Tinbergen (1963) wrote from a sociobiological perspective describing every action as having four separate kinds of ethological causes. These can be applied to motherhood in appreciating the types of infant care adopted by them.

- The proximal cause: the mother's poverty, her depression and fear of society's disapproval.

- The developmental cause: The mother is perhaps young with a negative experience of her own childhood. She may have a lack of role models in identifying what a caring mother is. This aligns with the ghosts in the nursery theory about parents own early childhood experiences and how this influences their role as a parent and their own maternal care giving roles (Fraiberg, 2019).

- The phylogenetic cause: She is a human but whose infant needs more physical and social support.

- The evolutionary function: the choice of abandoning an infant when they were deemed physically compromised and unable to thrive. The decision was based on long term care and needs met. (Hrdy, 1999b:697).

The first generation of family historians did not accept claims about maternal love existing, although the existence of love (or otherwise) was an aspect of their critical enquiries. This focus drew attention to the emotional mother–child relationship and the extent to how love and affection evolved. This evolved and changed over time as records of lived experiences and evolving expressions were documented (Knott, 2020). By evaluating the complexities of maternal love experiences and how they were expressed and documented, Bland (2019) provided autobiographical insights into the little-known history of children, born to black American servicemen and white British women during the Second World War. From 1942 to 1945 an estimated 2,000 children were born when American soldiers were stationed in Britain. Black GIs were forbidden to marry their pregnant girlfriends. Bland presents the narratives of more than forty children in her published book *Britain's Brown Babies*. One area relevant to infant loving care expressed and experienced were the family dynamics with illegitimate children. Many children believed, until they were quite old, that their grandparents were their birth parents. One story was about Stan, who was an unwanted infant by his 18-year-old mother. Subsequently he was adopted, loved and cared for by his maternal grandparents. Within this narrative it highlighted the recording of a loving relationship but also the challenges of grandparenting and raising an infant, alongside the local and national cultural attitude and prejudices of the time.

Roberts (1995a) evaluated that very few parents stressed or mentioned physical affection and tenderness explicitly or implicitly, but little recorded evidence did not mean it was absent. The period of 1850–1950 was associated with a shift from strict, authoritarian parenting to more affectionate, companionable parenting. At the turn of the twentieth century, parents considered and chose various approaches to parenting (Nelson and Holmes, 1997). Middle-class mothers reportedly became more involved with childcare, especially as care from the nanny or wet nurse declined, although upper-class parents supposedly remained formal, controlled and distant from their infants for a longer time than the middle classes. Working-class parents were also considered slower to change their methods, as they continued to be burdened with more children than resources, creating a need for strong discipline (Violett, 2018a). From this evaluation it seems the shift during this time was the desire and availability to be able to increase quality family time. There was also a further motivation to knowing their infants as a 'person', than previously acknowledged. Parents were seemingly wanting the best for their young children from birth.

However, Horn (1994) claimed parents have not always tried to do what is best for their children, with evidence supported by Shorter (1976) that infants were not prioritized within the context of their culture and furthermore many were continued to be harshly disciplined. Hendrik (1997) also argued that Pollock (1983) dismissed the view of the child within the cultural context. For Pollock, though, her research was intentionally focused on individuals through autobiography. The research of diaries of past centuries was therefore aimed to give voice to the individual rather than the cultural context. She agreed childcare was a complex system with parents anxious in their role. From her findings she evaluated discourses did include forms of affection and infant care. It was therefore dependent on what was being researched and what micro stories listened to (Pollock, 1983).

In the late eighteenth century, as the unpaid work performed by Western mothers emerged as something worthy of discussion, a clear image of the good mother was created. She was portrayed as a selfless, tender, full of love and ever devoted mother to her offspring. Violett (2018) highlighted Thompson's (1970) analysis of Edwardian oral history interviews. The relevant sources included affection, as all participants were asked whether their parents were affectionate (Hendrick, 1997b:18). The following examples were from working-class interviewees.

Parent: Born in 1893, affection was not only present, but expected:
'you had to show all affection. Oh yes, all right, you just all liked each other'.
Implied that his parents were not strict, unlike those of a teacher, born in 1902. Her parents were affectionate towards her, but her mother was very displeased when her daughter got dirty, and would send her to bed if she misbehaved, demonstrating a blend of old and new ideas about raising young children
A lower middle-class parent, described as friendly who spent a lot of time with him, but were not particularly affectionate towards him. (Violett, 2018a:1)

Thompson himself noted that smaller working-class families had more time for affection and less need for severe discipline, so perhaps having less or only one child had some influence on how they were treated in the family dynamic.

Violett (2018b) researched one-child families and revealed the power of the stereotype that they received unusual levels of love and attention from their parents. Parental affection at the turn of the twentieth century had less to do with class, family size, geography and age, and more to do with parents' individual personalities. This in part supports Burnett (1984) autobiographical account of Katie Taylor, who reflected during the late nineteenth century about her unconditional love for her mother. Her autobiography depicted the life of an agricultural labourer's daughter, the fourteenth of fifteen children. Whilst their family life was surrounded by poverty and lacking material goods there was a sense of a loving family. She portrayed the pain her mother felt with the loss of a child and how unusual for her, she had spoken to her vicar because the coffin was not allowed to enter the church, due to the doctor's statement of diphtheria (Burnett, 1984:292).

My mother was such a good humble little woman although I loved her and pitied her, I knew I could always depend on her love and support. (Burnett, 1984:292)

The growth of psychological expertise in the twentieth century led parents to concern about aspects of life that elicited little thought in the past, such as children's posture, sleep habits, siblings bonds and psychological well-being.

Care relationships in the twentieth century

Since the late nineteenth century, every generation has had experts advocating a parenting style they claim is supported by science, only to be challenged by alternative sources claiming scientific validation for their approach (Levine, 1987).

It was not until the twentieth century that conflicts among child-rearing experts became increasingly known to parents, responding, and selectively adopting certain styles of parenting. Behaviourists, such as the psychologist

FIGURE 7.2 A kiss for baby Anne, Mary Cassatt (*c.* 1897).

Watson, advised mothers to avoid hugging, kissing or playing with their infants. He advised rigid schedule feeding and sleeping, in developing a young child's developing self-control. During the same time, Spock purported a more loving relationship between mother and infants, but also worried intensely about the dangers of maternal over-involvement. What linked these contrasting viewpoints was a fear that any dysfunction in mother–child relationships would lead to lifelong psychological instabilities to future relationships (Cunningham, 2017; Mahood, 1980).

This period was viewed as the century of the child. Infants were constructed and conceived by parents as aspiring to be physically fit and in a loving relationship. They were recommended to be in homes where mothers were ever present, rearing their infants (Cunningham, 2017; Key, 2019).

Infant care relationships and institutions

Prior to the 1900s there was little research on attachment, with the belief that infants themselves either needed or give human love. John Locke (1690) and John Watson (1928), both behaviourists, believed infants were born as blank slates with the environment shaping them. This contrasted with psychoanalysis, which placed a high importance of loving relationships in understanding infants and developing healthy social emotional behaviour (Bowlby, 1969).

From the beginning of the twentieth century infant welfare services developed alongside educational programmes for working-class mothers. The first 'School for Mothers' opened in St Pancras in 1907 and by 1913 a hundred and fifty schools were teaching 'mothercraft'. The main aim of these schools was the belief that mothers' ignorance, rather than poverty, was to blame for malnutrition of their infants. Maternity and child welfare centres increased from 650 in 1915 to 1278 in 1918.

The Maternity and Child Welfare Act 1918 made it compulsory for local authorities to establish these centres; however, whilst this ensured that all pre-school children were examined, treatment continued to be more of a problem for women who did not work. They were not eligible for free medical care, unlike their insured husbands who paid through their wages into the National Insurance scheme. Children's physical condition also remained a concern when they entered school at five years old, with a third of all children needing treatment in 1920. This was because prior to attending they had been left untreated. This was to some extent due to the lack of services offered to infants after eighteen months and before they went to school at five years old. It culminated in a susceptible period of being left unseen by professionals and therefore untreated for infectious diseases. The infants were too old to attend the infant welfare centres and too young for the School Medical Service (Whitbread, 1972). The infant welfare centres were the responsibility of the Ministry of Health, and, although it tried to extend these services, including ante-natal clinics, the legislation remained permissive regarding some services. The Ministry could not force Local Authorities to offer all possible services. In the 1930s some Local Authorities offered an increase to services, but access to services remained diverse with some providing free whilst others charged through a means-testing system. Some areas provided free services such as ante- and post-natal clinics and health visiting. However, hospital care remained a concern, particularly for those infants remaining and living in care beyond the parental home (Cole, 2015; Whitbread, 1972).

Rene Spitz (1945) researched infants admitted to a hospital setting. He observed that in a short period an infant development decline was observable. He argued this decline was contributed by the differing infant care received during their time at the hospital. Infants often received medical and physical care in a clinical and procedural fashion, provided by the nurses, rather than the maternal care of touch, attention during feeding and attention they had received by their mother. After a three-month separation from the infant's mother, he evaluated that major development had ceased within the infant. The infants became observably passive, not attempting to roll over or sit up. Similar findings were also observed by Emmi Pickler, who had observed infants living within Hungarian orphanages (1970). As a psychoanalyst, Spitz carried out research from the 1930s through to the 1940s on the effects of maternal deprivation and hospitalization with infants, particularly those who were institutionalized for long periods and deprived of substitute maternal care. He primarily studied infants who had experienced abrupt, long-term separation from their primary caregiver, including those caregivers who had been incarcerated. Spitz (1946) described infant responses and reactions of grief, anger and apathy to partial emotional deprivation. He proposed that when the loved object is returned to the child within three to five months of age, recovery is prompt, but after five months, an infant will show symptoms of increasingly serious deterioration. Although the accuracy of documentation, correlation and causation was inconsistent and critiqued, Spitz's work remained valuable to understanding infant care and questioning the benefits of institutional care (Rosmalen et al., 2020; Wright, 1987).

John Bowlby developed an attachment theory that was popularized from the 1940s during a time when clinical experimental psychology was dominated by ideas from Sigmund Freud's psychoanalytic theory and John Watson's behaviourism. although they were very different in their views.

Food was perceived as a significant factor in the emotional relationships between a significant care.

Harry Harlow (1950s), an animal psychologist, studied monkeys and shifted his focus from learning to love, inspired by Rene Spitz's observational studies with infant care in hospital. For Harlow the initial biological drive to seek attachment is evident, even if it is not responsive and reciprocal but simply physically present. Attachment was characterized by specific behaviours in infants, such as seeking proximity to the attachment figure when they had become upset or threatened (Bowlby, 1969; Van der Horst et al., 2008). Harlow's explanation was that attachment developed when the carer offered a tactile object, such as a soft cloth, suggesting infants have an innate (biological) need to touch and cling to something for emotional comfort. He studied monkeys in the famous wire mother and cloth experiment, disputing affection and mother attachment was primarily focused around receiving food. This was during a similar period when Harry Bakwin's (1942) care of children in Bellevue Hospital (US) and made links with high mortality rates and contact. Initially mortality rates were thought to be due to malnutrition and infection at the hospital. Therefore, to avoid cross infection the open ward had been replaced by small cubicle rooms in which masked hooded and scrub nurses and physicians moved cautiously about in fear of spreading the bacteria. The infants received a high-calorie diet, but they still only gained weight once they were discharged home. Psychological neglect and a lack of mothering in the sterile environment on the wards were contributing to the health decline of infants. Therefore, nurseries were organized to encourage mothers and primary carers to regularly cuddle, pick up and play with their infants, despite the increased possibility of infection. Consequently, mortality rates for infants under one year of age fell sharply. During the 1950s James Robertson filmed the reactions of young children to hospital admission and in the 1960s, with his wife Joyce, recorded reactions of children subjected to separation. During the Second World War the effects of separation had been studied by Britton who had been dealing with the difficult behaviour of evacuated children (Winnicott and Britton, 1957). In the 1950s this was extended with the Robertsons' study (1958) on hospital and social care.

The Robertsons (1969) wanted to study the impact of separation on children and focused on four children – Kate, Thomas, Jane and Lucy – aged between eighteen months and two and a half years old. The Robertsons recorded their behaviour and filmed them along with a fifth child, John, who was admitted to a residential nursery in similar circumstances. They evaluated the young children, separated from their mothers, experienced a range of emotions including sadness and aggression, whilst noting a positive caring environment could mitigate almost all adverse reactions to separation. In all the cases studied there was an initial adaptation to the new environment followed by periods of grief and anger. The foster children demonstrated fluctuating emotions between the foster mother and their own mother. In John's case his behaviour difficulties were much more severe and prolonged with his return home. The long-term impact of his experience was a fear of separation from his mother and episodes of aggression towards his mother. This remained for months after returning home.

Contemplative question

Reflect on the following procedures based in England and discuss how these relate today. Consider these procedures during the pandemic and how COVID has impacted on visitation hours. What are your thoughts about the short- and long-term implications of paediatric care in hospitals?

Visiting hours: London Hospitals (Munro-Davies, 1949)

Guy's Hospital, Sundays, 2–4 pm

St Bartholomew's, Wednesdays 2–3:30 pm

Westminster Hospital, Wednesdays 2–3 pm, Sundays 2–3 pm

St Thomas's Hospital, first month no visits, parents could see children asleep 7–8 pm

West London Hospital, no visiting

Charing Cross Hospital, Sundays, 3–4 pm

London Hospital, under 3 years old, no visits, but parents could see children through partitions. Over 3 years old, twice weekly. (Bower and Trowell, 2002:25)

Support and care beyond the home

In addition to hospital care the lives of infants and children in residential homes remained largely invisible until the work of Marjory Allen in the 1940s. Whilst the focus has been on hospital care this legislation was valuable in recognizing the shift in social care. She was largely responsible for imposing the government to establish a committee, the Curtis Committee (1946), to look at the lives of children in these residential, institutional care settings.

The Committee's conclusions focused on three areas:

- Absence of a single centralized authority responsible for deprived children

- The lack of properly trained staff

- An insensitive treatment and sometimes excessive discipline towards children.

The Committee did not strongly criticize the general running of these homes or the discipline within them, but many of the comments portrayed a bleak picture about institutional life for infants and young children. The Children Act 1948 was subsequently passed, putting into effect the findings of the Committee and finally abolishing the Poor Law legislation. The Act resulted in the organization of Children's Departments within local authorities and the appointment of a Children's Officer (who were mainly women) and Children's Committees. The emphasis changed from placing children in residential care to fostering, also known as boarding-out, to offering as near a normal home life as possible. Reinstatement of infants and children in care to their natural parents was considered favourable, with adoption being the next closest and desirable form of home care for young children (Higginbotham, 2017; Whitbread, 1972).

Contemplative question

Read the following case study and discuss in relation to infant care, love and communication.

What are the ethical implications of this case study regarding institutional infant care?

Contemplative case study

In Ontario at the beginning of the 20th century a mother gave birth to five girls. The Dionne quintuplets were born in Ontario Canada in 1936 and were the first known case of quintuplets.

The Ontario government removed the babies from their home as they were considered poor working-class parents allegedly not able to care for the still vulnerable infants. They were made wards of the state, raised in a hospital in their hometown. It was built, especially to house them and was known as Quintland.

The girls were raised according to the latest scientific knowledge, with a focus on cleanliness and regularity of feeding times and sleeps. In this arrangement the medical professionals controlled the knowledge about raising young children.

Quintland became a tourist attraction, and the general public were allowed to observe the children at set times during the day.

The state argued that it was acting in the best interests of the children and furthermore served the interests of the state, encouraging parents to rear their children in a more scientific way of the future.

Nine years later the quintuplets' parents won a custody of their children and were able to take them home and away from Quintland. Their story is told through their own autobiographies and provides the dichotomy between state intervention and family life. (Brough et al., 1965; Soucy, 1997)

Connections with contemporary care practice

Infants in England tend to spend less time in foster care and secure a family quicker through adoption than older children. If possible, the mother will attend a foster family with their infant if the situation is temporary in a bid to retain them together. Today infants who are in the care system from a very young age are often moved to foster carers, whilst the courts reach a decision about who will care for them in the long term. Research has shown that too many carers and disruptions have a negative impact on a child's mental health and development. Early permanence removes this disruption by placing a child early on with foster carers who would go on to adopt them, if the court decides that is in the child's best interests. This means that, if the court agrees an adoption plan, the child has a seamless transition from foster care to adoption, without having to move from a foster home where they have settled to a new adoptive family. A secure, consistent family environment is the aspiration for all infants and young children in care (Coram adoption, nd).

Attachment and care: Linking theory to everyday care practices

From the mid-twentieth century attachment theorists have developed a model of parent–child relationships from a broad theoretical base that includes ethology, cognitive psychology and control systems (Ainsworth et al., 1979; Bowlby, 1969). John Bowlby was particularly interested in identifying the nature, significance and function of an infant's emotional closeness to their parent. Although initially the theory had its roots in clinical observations of children who experienced severely compromised relationships, it has been applied to modern day as a model for normal and abnormal development. From a psychological perspective, it focuses on the extent to which the relationship provides the infant and young child with protection against harm, with a sense of emotional security. The theory proposes that the quality of care provided, particularly sensitivity and responsiveness, leads to a secure attachment (Bowlby, 1969). The way infants develop emotionally is argued to be determined predominately by the sensitivity and characteristics of their parent(s) or primary carer. The more sensitive and reliable, the more secure attachment flourishes with the infant. Tuning into an infant's behaviour and feelings creates opportunities for bonding experiences and enables the infant to regulate their own emotions and begin to make sense of how they feel about themselves. However, attachment theorists use the term 'pathway' to reinforce the idea that early attachment experiences, including those lacking experiences can influence but not determine later development. Furthermore Rutter (2002) argued anti-social behaviour was not linked to maternal deprivation as such but influenced by family discord. The importance of these refinements of the maternal deprivation hypothesis was to reposition it as a vulnerability factor, rather than a causative agent, with several varied influences determining the projected life of the infant (Norman, 2019).

In observing secure attachments rather than waiting until the infant was an adult and asking retrospectively, Ainsworth (1979) drew on what she termed the Strange Situation. This was developed as way to understand the value of close relationships and emotional attachments. Ainsworth asked if the attachment of infant to mother was secure, insecure, disorganized or ambivalent. Ainsworth's Strange Situation (1979) used structured observational research to measure and assess the quality of attachment. The research had eight predetermined conditions, including the mother leaving the child, for a short while, to play with available toys in the presence of a stranger and alone and the mother returning to the child. The results highlighted the role of the mother, parent or main carer and their consistent caring behaviour in determining the quality of attachment (Cohen and Waite-Shipansky, 2017).

Physical infant care, crying and communication

In the late nineteenth century, many children under five were suffocated by bed clothes, overlaid or sacrificed. Very little physical care would be carried out and new-born infants were put in garments and moved and touched as little as possible. They were placed in a cot containing hot water bottles, wrapped in a flannel. The advice was for the infant to not sleep in their mother's bed because it was very likely to suffocate by covering. Practically it was almost impossible to persuade the poor to provide a separate cot for the infant. Many lived in close accommodation to neighbours having moved from rural to urban areas, and the need to quieten the crying infant was immense during the night (Coles, 2015).

In *Mrs William Parkes, Domestic Duties; or, Instructions to Young Married Ladies, on the Management of Their Households, and The Regulation of Their Conduct in the Various Relations and Duties of Married Life* (1825), she analysed different types of infant cries;

- short and ranging due to hunger

- continued and drawn out was for pain of some sort

- contented baby quietly and placidly closed eyes

Connections with contemporary care practices

We now know infant vocalization comes in many forms and pitched differently depending on their needs. Crying, particularly persistent crying, is a noise somehow divorced from the infant and to an adult ear is a noise that needs to be stopped by whatever means necessary. However, what is more beneficial is tuning into the cry and listening, attempting to decode the crying, finding out what they are trying to say vocally. The reasons for communicative crying we recognize today are very similar to those recognized in 1825.

- Hunger
- Thirst
- Discomfort
- Loneliness and anxiety
- Too hot/cold
- Over stimulation
- Colds
- Allergies
- Pain (Norman, 2019).

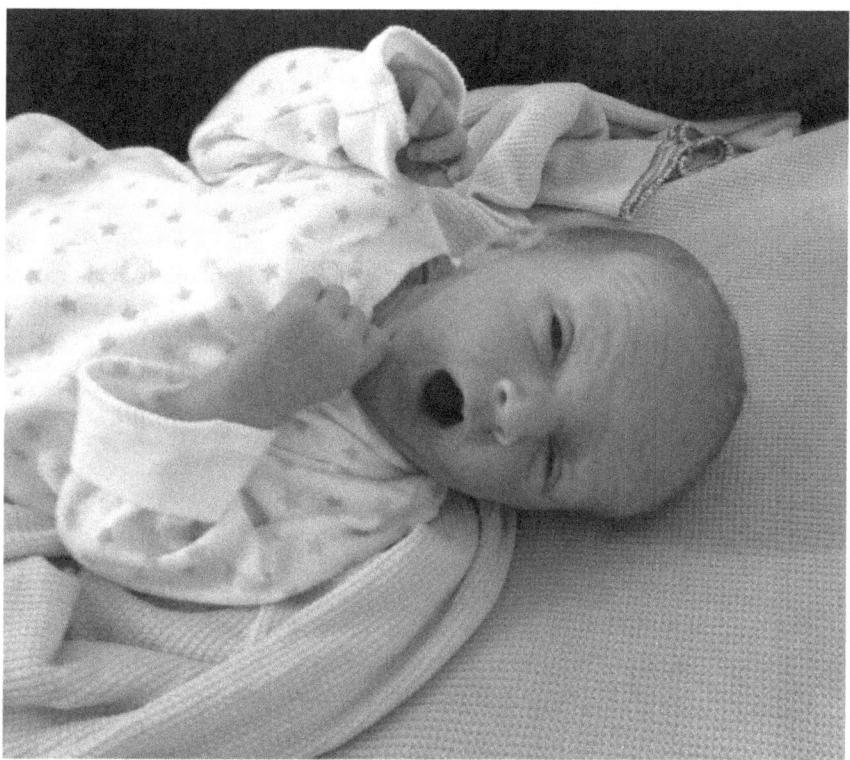

FIGURE 7.3 Communicating.

Contemplative case study: Voices of care

Crying and Communication

Bathing, as part of an infant's routine was carried out by initially bathing in tepid water, gradually getting colder and colder as the infant gets used to it. Lively singing accompanied the experience, so the cold water was associated with the experience. Cold water to wash physically, morally bracing cold water. This was to aid nappy rash and rainwater washes were also carried out. In 1840 the infant was regularly put in clean clothes, at least a dozen times. This was reduced by three months of age, so by four months you can teach your child to be clean. The mothers disgrace remedies for their child's bed wetting were to sleep on straw as well as to be frequently flogged with a stick brush. (Barrett, 1875:111)

During the twentieth century crying was not just about emotions but a form of language between the carer and infant. As an educator and teacher Mikhail Bakhtin's approach to language was shared with his colleague Voloshinov (1895–1936). It highlighted language as taking place in social contexts that are laden with meanings, relating it to his theory of dialogism. Though Bakhtin did not specifically focus on early years development, he did refer to the role of language in a young child's life and this is argued to connect to the emotional communication and the way language is interpreted (White, 2015).

From the lips of those close to him ... they are the words that for the first time determine his personality from outside. The child begins to see himself through his mother's eyes and begins to speak about himself in his mother's emotional volitional tones. (Bakhtin, 1990 in White, 2015: 49–50)

Language is the way an infant begins to view themselves and their personality. Language is therefore a lifelong journey of ideological becoming rather than transmitting language as a purpose for learning codes. For Bakhtin what is learned is less to do with linguistic and cognitive functioning but the development of the creative personality as an infant engages with a multifaceted and social world (Bakhtin, 1981).

Bakhtin stressed language was not sequential or a universal hierarchal pattern, as suggested by popular scientists. It was more of a fluid narrative representing voices through discourses. Language for him contained both revealing and concealing meanings, presented in the self in many forms. Therefore, meaning is not fixed and exists within and between living spaces. The words spoken are therefore influenced by the values of those involved and the unspoken language, gestures, facial expressions, body language all contribute towards social language (White, 2015).

Connections with contemporary infant care practices

During the mid-twentieth century Colwyn Trevarthen (1993) also considered infants were born with the readiness to know another human and engage with them. He evaluated interactions between carers as mutual, with infants taking the lead within the interaction rather than simply responding to their carer's behaviour. Colwyn Trevarthen and Lynne Murray (1993) described this mutual interaction as proto conversations between infant and carer turn taking experience. Through turn taking the carer can adapt their interactive behaviour to the rhythms of their infant. It encourages the infant to lead the interaction, therefore tuning in to their infant in an emotionally communicative way (Degtardi and Davis, 2008). By understanding how close connections have developed throughout history and the approaches taken it enables a reflexive approach to be taken when communicating and responding to infant care needs.

Conclusion: A personal note

The focus of this chapter has been the shift from family to community care, specifically the care in hospitals and the significant studies and observations that took part in leading change at policy and practice level. Many early years professionals would be familiar with the Robertsons, and this is a timely reminder of the significance of their work, alongside Bowlby and Spitz. This chapter therefore connects historical practices of institutional care received beyond the home with present day care. It also offers a fresh perspective to the value of observation, research and cross-disciplinary approaches for change to occur and how this connects to contemporary practice.

CHAPTER EIGHT

Edu-care and play

Introduction and context

Thinking and understanding about play pedagogies features throughout childhood studies programmes as well as those working with infants and young children. Caring through a learning and playful approach unites and differentiates various early years curriculums both nationally and internationally when examining and comparing them. This chapter explores and contributes to the studies and researched areas of edu-care and play with infants. By focusing on selected studies, relationships will be made between health and play pedagogies. The care approaches will be contextualized within settings, including dame schools and the resources offered to young infants. Furthermore Jean-Jacques Rousseau, Friedrich *Froebel* and more contemporary works of Margaret and Rachel McMillan and Susan Isaacs will widen the discussion and value of play. Finally, in the chapter the role of the professional carer will then be discussed, with a focus to the shifts in care within educational settings.

> The Key Person Approach is a way of working in nurseries in which the whole focus and organisation is aimed at enabling and supporting close attachments between individual children and individual nursery staff. The Key Person approach is an involvement, an individual and reciprocal commitment between a member of staff and a family. It is an approach that has clear benefits for all involved. (Elfer, Goldschmied and Selleck, 2011:18)

Parents and out of care

In 2020 an English social media Twitter thread asked whether grandparents should regularly look after their infant throughout the day and overnight whilst the mother returned to work. Of the eighty-three respondents everyone not only agreed but enthused this was a great idea. The responding parents considered it was an optimum time for the grandparents to potentially form close relationships with their grandchildren as well as an incentive for the mother because she would be more financially secure (assuming the parents were not giving the grandparents any money). The motives for the mother wanting to return to work were mentioned, although this was to a lesser extent and only three respondents cited professional care such as childminders as an option. Whilst it is considered a typical thread often found on social media sites, it emphasizes the contemporary discourses around family childcare arrangements and the reliance and significance of extended family members and paid childcare. McCarthy (2020) evaluated that during the Second World War there were some opportunities for parents to occasionally take their infant into work whilst they continued to be employed. However, many employers were less accommodating and without family support an extra shift was unachievable. Subsequently a lack of opportunities to make a little more money for the family income was often challenging. A further option was accessing day nurseries and whilst these are a well-established feature of early years today, they were a service developed as a cultural response to the needs of the time. For some parents they were not always a preferable choice.

During the mid-twentieth century nursery crèche places were expanded and the government provided subsidies with the growing demand for childcare. By 1918 in England 160 state-funded crèches were in operation, with room to accommodate 7,000 children between the times of 8:00 am and 7:00 pm, five days a week, with an additional half a day on Sunday and some overnight stays if needed. The crèches were often located near women's homes rather than their workplaces. They were purpose-built with attractive outdoor spaces, and had equipment included such as cots (Hardyment, 2007). Some premises were originally public houses and had been changed to nurseries or infant welfare centres. Nursery crèches were often managed by a matron in charge who advocated infants should receive good hygiene, fresh air and a managed diet (Whitbread, 1972). Typically, this included meat, potatoes and stewed fruit, as well as regularly providing milk. The children were examined on arrival and received a bath (McCarthy, 2020). They were dressed in nursery clothing whilst their own clothes were disinfected, and these were returned to the children when they were collected by their parents. Outdoor engagement was encouraged, and this included visits to the local park, or a rooftop play area. Mothers who breast-fed were invited to come in at lunch and eat with their babies. This appeared an idyllic option for many families and not too dissimilar to today in some of the practices mentioned, providing a much-needed service. However, there were some negative aspects of day nursery which continued to cause a barrier for many mothers to access this nursery service. Predominately, strict rules were administered by the matrons. They were also considered to have health concerns with the breakout of infections, such as measles whooping cough and meningitis. Matrons priorities were often around reducing infection and therefore a health focus took precedence, with much less concern about being welcoming and warm towards the infants and their families (Whitbread, 1972).

Out of care in history

By understanding the shift from early years home care to nursery crèches and nursery schools an exploration of dame schools provides an appropriate beginning. The precise origins of dame schools are unknown. They were generally evolved from a demand for accessible early childhood education for older children and care for infants. They were often initiated as a response to parents of labouring classes in needing and accessing cheap, convenient

FIGURE 8.1 Caring and teaching in private homes.

childcare. School dames worked with small groups of children, in the dame's home, wherever a demand existed. Their own qualifications were accepted, although this varied depending on who asked (Gathorne-Hardy, 1973). They tended to be generally female, middle-class widows and spinsters or young, unmarried women who needed additional income. Whilst the women in charge might be a homely and kindly person or crippled for factory work there were others who could be uncaring and unscrupulous.

Dame schools were therefore deemed as cheap, accessible childcare, frequently offered by a neighbour and in some instances would take as many young children and infants as possible. Dame schools were not an organization and there was not an interconnected group, run by independent women within their own local areas. As they were independently established and delivered the conditions varied. Some dame schools were based in crowded rooms or in a cellar that was unventilated and generally unhealthy and dirty. Dame schools were largely affected by the industrialization of the nineteenth century. As an increasing number of parents were involved in wage labour at factories the rise of dame schools came to be viewed as an option to access affordable day care. Their sole purpose was childcare, rather than educational purposes. However, this did continue to vary in relation to the dame herself (Higginson, 1974).

With the unregulated and irregular delivery of childcare and education dame schools gradually reduced, replaced by baby classes in infant schools.

FIGURE 8.2 "A Dame's School'. In the 1887. The Dame School, Frederick George Cotman (1887) Public Domain Material https://www.wikiart.org/en/frederick-george-cotman/ the-dame-school-1887 Accessed 17 April 2021.

During 1870 over 19,000 of infants to three years were placed in baby classes. Skilled workers trained as public nurses and provided nursery accommodation, deemed the most appropriate form of infant care. In practice many infants in their classrooms were often penned into their seats to contain and manage them. As the entry number of infants continued to rise and overcrowding occurred, the typical ratio was twenty infants to a matron and a female assistant. The nursery places were financially self-supporting, even though most of the accommodation were rent-free. Therefore, the calculated needs charged was £5 a day for a minimum of twenty infants to cover expenses. This included meal breaks and sometimes rent (Whitbread, 1972).

In the late nineteenth century, it was typical for there to be a class of fifty to sixty children between two and five years old, left in charge with a girl of thirteen to fourteen years old. The resources for the nursery remained expensive too, and there was therefore a pressure from parents to 'educate' their children academically. Parents paying for the service wanted their children to acquire academic knowledge early, referred to as payment by results. The working class were not given the opportunity to express themselves through the creative arts, and this was considered inappropriate for children of the lower classes. However, there were European approaches already developing including Montessori and Froebel who had a much more child-centred philosophy to play and care, particularly with infants (Cunningham, 2017:158).

Policy and care

The nineteenth century saw the beginning of voluntary day nurseries in 1850 provided by charitable bodies in direct response to the poor standards of care offered by child minders. From as early as the 1870s there was a demand that local authorities should provide nurseries and maintain a register of childminders. The Nurseries and Childminders Act (1948) was passed, and therefore private day care was managed under the local authority control for the first time. This Act was amended in 1968 to require childminders to register, nearly 100 years after this was first demanded (McNamee, 2016).

The 1948 Act was passed as the National Health Service of the England (NHS) formed and the 'welfare state' was taking shape. Child welfare was an integral part of this broad democratic vision.

The Education Act 1944, the foundation of the NHS in 1948 and the Children's Act 1948 set up systems of prevention and interventions across the country. The state also sought to support children within families through education, housing, health and social services, rather than removal. This mirrors the multi-professional early years' services existing today (Leach, 2018).

By 1941 in the UK three kinds of provision were available to families

1   Full-time nurseries, supervised by a matron, were open between 12 and 15 hours a day. This was catered for infants from a few months to five years old. A trained schoolteacher was available for those children over two and half years.

2   Part-time nursery class was managed under a teacher and open during normal school hours with children between two and five years.

3   Admission age in infant schools was lowered to two years, therefore becoming an alternative provision (McCarthy, 2020a).

There was a clear preference for nurseries and nursery classes rather than childminders during this time. However as from the description above professionals worked together and at times there was discord between matrons and nursery teachers, regarding the emphasis on health and education in early years settings (Davis, 2014). Middle-class families also accessed a further alternative provision of Au Pairs, these being a cheap untrained substitute for a Norland Nanny or childminder (Gathorne-Hardy (1973).

Contemplative case study: Training options

This letter provided information regarding the type of training and provision during 1941, highlighting the children's needs during the war.

- *Provision must be made to care for these children while their mothers are at work. The greatest single contribution to the problem must be from the women of the district themselves who must between them carry out the two tasks of looking after their children and working in the factories. Those who cannot go to the factory will help those who can. It is the responsibility of the maternity a child welfare and local education authority to secure other arrangements for their children. It is the responsibility and duty of the nation, which at this time needs no emphasis provision of wartime nurseries nursery classes of children under 5.*

- *It is hoped private arrangements with friends or relatives for the care of their children will be sought and available during the time. Nursery recruitment will be targeted 16- and 20-years women sought as future careers, on probationary workers, as well as women of over 30 years.*

- *Women of 20 to 30 years who cannot take up labour and national service may be recruited.*

- *Childcare Training: The courses of instruction for the childcare reserve will be widely advertised in the area.*

- *Interviews should be carried out by local authorities to judge suitability, with a small payment 10 shillings per week allocate. The Board of Education should carry out an oral examination. If a written exam is set, then it will be organised by the National Council or local HM inspectors.*

- *Breakfast and after school clubs will be available ... in schools, school canteens and other centres.* (Mass observation, 1941)

The latter part of the twentieth century saw the play group movement develop in England and in 1961, with the efforts of Mrs Bella Tutaev, became a national movement. This form of childcare was much more parent-centred than previously and therefore formed an alternative service to education and health already being offered in the community. The Nuffield foundation gave a grant of £1,500 in 1962 and the Department of Education and Science £3,000 for three years. The movement spread quickly and by 1971 there were about 7,000 playgroups to 170,000 children. They were not considered nursery schools but similarly were led by a qualified supervisor. The groups accommodated six to thirty children, between two and four years who played together regularly attending several weekly sessions. The parents, generally mothers, actively supported the movement, and their active attendance was integral to the service. They assisted on a rota and participation as a volunteer was considered important. The sessions were often short, and a small payment was requested as a contribution to refreshments, equipment or the rental of the accommodation. Mothers accessed the playgroup as a way of connecting and supporting each other in the care of their young children (Crow, 2013). For the working class a further service was pioneered by Save the Children, with 120 funded groups formed by 1971. These were known as The One O'clock Club. They were not in competition with other forms of childcare, but rather a stopgap facility for socialization between parents and an opportunity for children to socially play, meeting a social need in the community (Whitbread, 1972).

Young children, care and education: The Children Act 1989

This Act asserts that 'the child is a person and not an object of concern' and put into place a far-reaching reform of existing childcare law. The welfare of the child is the 'paramount consideration', and although the emphasis is on 'listening to children', children were not involved or consulted.

The Act represented a change in attitude and was concerned with three key areas:

- Parental responsibility and rights

- Support for children and their families

- Partnership between parents and educators in early years settings beyond the home.

The Act also required local authorities to inspect day care premises annually as a condition of continuing registration and set quotas of children that each childminder could accept. However, the vision of this later Act was much more limited than its 1948 predecessor, despite the concern of both the family and its relationship with the local authority and the state (Whitbread, 1972). Whilst child welfare was an integral part of this broad democratic vision of 1948, it was argued that the Child Act 1989 had an increased closed view of the family as a private institution. This reflected the political ethos of individualism in society during this period. In advocating for the voice of the infant and young child, prioritizing their health, play and care pioneers throughout history is discussed.

Looking back: Key nursery pioneers, play and edu-care

In 1569 children's games was depicted by Pieter Brugel in his painting depicting a forgotten folk culture of Belgium life. It portrays the variety of amusement enjoyed by young people and young children, including barrel play, ring games and small gatherings. Eakins also depicted paintings between 1870 and 1870 with two-year-old Ella Crowell phasing out of her baby toys into the world of language, with the visible painted alphabet blocks played with. These paintings therefore illustrated the interest and focus of toys with infants at play, revealing the presence of 'childhood' often disregarded during the period they were painted.

The first writings of play were related to education and with a role in skills acquisition, playing with tools for a purpose (Pollock, 1983). Puritan tradition in northern Europe and America tended to have a negative view of children with the thought of them having original sin. Play was therefore viewed as linked to the animal expression of instinctive behaviours and needed to be restructured or channelled to appropriate civilization and civilizing activities. A more positive focus on play came from Rousseau's view of infants and children, with pure souls but perverted by the ills of society. In the eighteenth century Rousseau wrote *Emile*, a treatise, using the medium of the novel to dramatize his ideas to access and reach out to

FIGURE 8.3 Children playing on the beach 1884.

a wide audience. He discussed the nature of education and served as the inspiration for what became a new national system of child-rearing and education (Cunningham, 2017). He focused on the environmental view of the child, being different to adults with an innocence, slow to mature. He believed they were entitled to freedom and happiness and were naturally good. The five stages begin with stage one, infancy birth to two years and stage one concludes with weaning (Gathorne-Hardy, 1973).

The only habit the child should be allowed to acquire is to contract none ... freedom and the exercise of his powers, by allowing his body its natural habits and accustoming him always to be his own master and follow the dictates of his will as soon as he has a will of his own. (Émile, Book 1 – translation by Boyd, 1956: 23; Everyman edn: 30)

In stage 2

'The age of Nature' (two to 12). The second stage, from two to ten or twelve, is 'the age of Nature'. During this time, the child receives only a 'negative education': no moral instruction, no verbal learning. He sets out the most important rule of education: 'Do not save time, but lose it ... The mind should be left undisturbed till its faculties have developed'. (Everyman edn.: 57; Boyd: 41)

The purpose of education was at this stage to develop physical qualities, specifically the senses, but not the minds, with play viewed as a natural expression of childhood that should be fostered (Wokler, 1995).

Linda Pollock (1983), in *Forgotten Children* (p. 236), evaluated that play was very often recorded more in the eighteenth and nineteenth centuries. Diaries included aspects of play but were often met with some disapproval. A mother from 1663 to 1728 provided paints, with an emphasis on learning rather than playing which was not something to be encouraged. Another entry from 1601 to 1658 noted the value of learning, viewing play as idol and to be avoided. Other diaries were less disapproving and met with amusement regarding play.

Contemplative case study: Examples of play

Linda Pollock's (1983) findings from her examination of diaries in the sixteenth and seventeenth centuries featured play intermittently.

Jefferay 1591 to 1675 (p.237) wrote about rambles in the wood, fantasy play and role play. He discussed that children went out to play with another child by three years of age. In the 17th century snowboarding, fishing and cricket over the common was mentioned with flower making carried out with older children. The 18th century provided more detail with girls looking after infants and how so they got accustomed regarding the usefulness of their role.

Braithwaite's 1788 to 1859 Anna Braithwaite born Anna Lloyd (27 December 1788 – 18 December 1859: p.137, 238) was a prominent English Quaker minister. They described a child of three years being chased by pigs into the house. At three years old the child was also described as demanding their parents to help with buildings constructed with bricks. In another diary a child of two and half years was described as playing at being a gardener lamplighter or engine driver. (Pollock, 1983:237)

Inspirational pioneers such as Friedrich Froebel sought an alternative view of play, care, development and education. Froebel, influenced by Johann Pestalozzi (1746–1827), a Swiss educator, emphasized the role of practical experience in contact with objects. Friedrich Froebel's philosophical journey began with a focus on children in the middle years of childhood in 1817 but then focused on the younger children between the ages of two and seven years. The children's garden, the kindergarten and outdoors in its many forms were a key feature of Froebel. The latter part of his work and philosophical thinking centred around the pedagogy of infants and toddlers. He developed the value of mother songs and nursery songs in 1844. Friedrich Froebel's (1782–1852) philosophy of education was unique in that he advocated mutual respect and holistic learning. He promoted learning through experience and considered Mother Songs to be the initial stage in developing early physical skills of the body and senses. The print culture of the eighteenth century was over laying the oral tradition of verse, capturing a wealth of traditional nursery rhymes such as lullaby's nonsense and playground rhymes. *The Mother Song Book* (1844) was considered a family book with sections written specifically for mothers to engage with their infants. Latter sections were also written to include mothers and fathers to engage with their infants. It developed the relationship between parent and infant within the family context, with a reciprocal communication gaining a sense of belonging to their family, community and culture. He considered Mother Songs as a way of forming close supporting emotional relationships through actively engaging. The significance of this was his emphasis on creating care connections with the whole family, educators and the community. He also focused on the importance for infants to be able to move their body, limbs, hands and fingers introducing educational movement games with children who were able to walk and talk (Bruce, 2021). The purpose was also for the mother to gain a sense of rewarding responsibility in supporting the development of their infant in their care (Bruce, 2021).

> Indeed, mans whole development requires that his surroundings speak to him clearly ... So in words and songs the mother tries to express this and bring the life of his environment closer to him. (Froebel in Lilley, 1967:105)

A Froebelian philosophy engaging in The Mother Songs' principles and pedagogy included:

- Recognition of the uniqueness of each child's capacity and potential

- A holistic approach to learning which recognizes children as active, feeling and thinking human beings, seeing patterns and making connections

FIGURE 8.4 Baby lying on his mother's lap, reaching to hold a scarf, Mary Cassatt (1914).

- Individual and collaborative activity and play (Norman, 2019; Tovey, 2012).

Included in the Mother Songs were finger rhymes, which involved musical voice alongside finger manipulation to occur in unique ways.

Music is especially important, since the sounds which a child produces in singing ... serve to give creative expression to feelings and ideas. (Froebel in Lilley, 1967:113)

Finger rhymes in contemporary practice: What we know today

Actively engaging in a close relationship and using the same finger rhymes stimulate connections between brain neurons, therefore developing the capacity to increase brain development.

> Froebel believed by repeating and retelling the use of finger rhymes, using finger manipulation, forming close bonds.

This all contributed to the journey of more complex thinking and learning about literacy such as story making.

Play and psychology in the twentieth century

John Dewey (1859–1952) promoted a view that infants and young children learnt through experience and their education based on real-life situations. This promoted the idea that both the teachers and parents should encourage independent thought and experimentation to nurture both the infant's curiosity and their disposition. The central premise being for children to actively experience rather than passively learn. In the twentieth century infant play was conceived within a scientific lens; key theorists including Isaacs and Darwin explored the connection between psychoanalysis and play (Smith, 2010). Susan Isaacs (1885–1948) promoted the nursery school movement in her work around education and psychoanalysis. She drew on the value of the schoolteacher and the importance of observation and play (Isaacs, 1930). She was a British psychologist and educationalist whose work spanned the first half of the twentieth century (Mickelburgh, 2018). She came to education with a background in philosophy and psychology, and this influenced a great deal of her work with young children. Smith (1985) evaluated that Isaacs successfully integrated the increasing theoretical knowledge of child psychology with practice in both child-rearing practices and education (p. 17). Isaacs was known for the accessibility of her work for practitioners and parents. She wrote for a varied audience, including academic papers, books and columns in parenting journals. Isaacs's child-centred theories expanded on the work of other educationalists, such as Froebel's approach to active learning and Dewey's emphasis on social interaction, making them accessible to those working with children (Dryden et al., 2005; Pound, 2005; Isaacs, 1933). She believed adults needed to understand young children's play exploration. At the Malting House school, it provided a setting to facilitate children's development. The indoor space was richly resourced to stimulate learning through play. It included dressing up clothes, art and craft materials, beads, blocks, a typewriter and other play equipment (Isaacs, 1930). Comparable to Montessori's schools, the tables, chairs and cupboards were low down and easy to transport. There were mattresses and rugs for quiet play and resting. The main room opened onto the garden, where there was a playhouse, sand pit, tool shed, plots for gardening and one of the first climbing frames in Britain. Isaacs also believed in taking the children out of the setting. These trips were always purposeful and initiated by the children. The equipment was also chosen purposefully, intended to stimulate the child's powers of inquiry, learning and curiosity (Smith, 1985:64). Children were given the space to set up games and, where appropriate, to sustain them over long periods, rather than be rushed to tidy them away (Mickelburgh, 2018). Isaacs felt this promoted focus and patience. The children were expected to take responsibility for the nursery environment, including planning the lunches, setting the table and washing up (Isaacs, 1933). Isaacs believed children's play was a form of self-expression that enabled them both to release their real feelings safely and to rehearse ways of dealing with a range of emotions. Play was the vehicle for development, the 'breath of life to the child, since it is through play activities that he finds mental ease, and can work upon his wishes, fears and fantasies to integrate them into a living personality' (Isaacs, 1951:210).

Connections with contemporary care practices

According to Smith (1985), Isaacs's contributions to modern practice reside in her analysis about child-centred practice and play. She gave credence to this approach, contributing to its long-term influence and giving confidence to practitioners who were already following her ideas. These theories are now woven into contemporary early years practice and play, as demonstrated by international early years curriculum guidance. Through play opportunities infants and young children can express fears and relive anxious experiences.

Play and infant care connections

Truby King's approach to parenting, advocated by Mabel Liddiard, in her *Mother Craft Manual* (1928), assured mothers that strict regimes such as potty training would result in controlled obedience, recognition of authority and later respect for elders. This was a popular parenting style for both mothers and practitioners in the early twentieth century. However, the social nursery campaigner Margaret Macmillan took an alternative approach and believed that young children needed stimulation and nurture (Rowbotham, 1997).

FIGURE 8.5 Sensory path play.

Rachel and Margaret McMillan (1860–1931) were inspirational educators and politically aware of the link between health and play. Margaret and Rachel's work in Bradford convinced them that they should concentrate on trying to improve the physical and intellectual welfare of the 'slum child'. In 1892 Margaret joined Dr James Kerr, Bradford's school medical officer, to carry out the first medical inspection of elementary school children in Britain. Kerr and McMillan published a report on the medical problems that they had discovered. They then began a campaign to improve the health of children by arguing that local authorities should install bathrooms, improve ventilation and supply free school meals. The Open-Air Nursery School and Training Centre, set up by the McMillan sisters, Rachel and Margaret, opened in 1914. The expansion of nurseries envisaged after the Second World War never materialized, but McMillan continued to open and run her own nursery in Deptford. It was a hybrid approach, combining Michel's radical ideas of spontaneous development with the educationalist Myers (1913) enthusiasm for garden schools and implementing a regulatory school hygiene approach. The nursery school influenced both the state nurseries in Britain and the progressive school movement (Rowbotham, 2011).

In a radio broadcast in 1927 she described the children's play:

> Children aged between two and five arrived at 8.00am and went to small shelters, in a big garden where they had breakfast of Brown bread and oatmeal porridge with milk.
>
> They spent their day amidst animals with as much sunlight, colour, music and dancing as possible. The nursery cured them of rickets and anaemia and reduced the incidences of measles. (Rowbotham, 1997:137)

Their philosophy was that children learnt by exploring and would achieve their full potential through first-hand experience and active learning. They stressed the importance of free play, particularly with craft and water activities, and outdoor play, providing large and varied external areas for this.

In 1926 parents took their children to the open-air nursery and conveyed their child's experiences. They stated their children were allowed and enabled to engage in a period of doing, feeling and observing the world. The McMillan style was therefore about providing the child with all kinds of materials by means of which they could find their own way, with less restricted materials provided than other popular approaches advocated during the period (Rowbotham, 2011).

Connections with contemporary care practices

Views surrounding out of home infant care seem commonplace now, but these were unique to the teaching and evolving play methods generally used at the time. A holistic approach to children was developed with the importance of caring for and educating the whole child with the content of the social and economic circumstances, all of which must be underpinned by social health or sound health (McMillan, 1930).

Similarly, the Montessori colleges and Pen Green centre based in England today continue to promote professional training and research, together with the delivery of care and education. MacMillan also established the Rachel McMillan teacher training College in Deptford in 1930. She introduced a sociological perspective into teaching practice, so teachers were encouraged to know more about the communities and circumstances of the children and families in communities in which they were teaching. Teachers and parents were involved in home visits, advocated as a means of helping nursery workers gain insights into the children's experience at home. It also aided collaboration and created a multidisciplinary way of working to holistically meet children's needs (Bruce, 2021). When in 1914 the McMillan sisters decided to start an Open-Air Nursery School and Training Centre in Deptford there were thirty children at the school ranging in age from eighteen months to seven years. The open-air setting remains a popular aspect of child facilities today with the indoor being seamlessly connected to the outdoors by partitions, windows and connecting doors. Rachel McMillan, who was mainly responsible for the kindergarten, stated that in the first six months there was only one case of illness and, again, the health benefits of the outdoors are part of early years education beyond exercise (Simkin, 1997).

Conclusion: A personal note

This chapter aimed to bridge play and infant care in settings from the past to the present. As a chapter it was approached by selectively drawing on specific theories and pioneers in history, some from recent history and others from further back. It was also approached by reflecting on the pioneers who believed infancy and childcare should be child-/infant-centred, suggesting that traditional and popular behaviourist approaches be re-examined and re-focused with emphasis on infant and child agency within care and educational contexts. By highlighting the continuing importance and contribution of historical pioneers there is an appreciation and understanding with contemporary practice.

CHAPTER NINE

A cross-disciplinary approach to studying infants

Introduction and context

In this chapter I will include two disciplines: social anthropology and biography. These are considered valuable contributions to studying the historical perspectives of infant care. The cross-disciplinary topic of infant care will introduce relevant themes and offer a connection to some of the previous areas already discussed. Unpublished voices will also be included to bridge themes associated with infant care.

Initially Mead's anthropological findings during the early twentieth century will be discussed in relation to their relevance with contemporary to infant care. Communal living will also be explored as an alternative view towards infant care, and this way of living is deemed a stark contrast to contemporary living in the West. In discussing the kibbutz lifestyles it will demonstrate not only infant care as a group activity but also the ways infant care has been studied in the past. The three unpublished narratives will then present a snapshot about having infant care in the mid-twentieth century. They position and begin their story from pregnancy, continuing with a narrative on key themes about caring for their infant(s.) This closes with a reflection about the value of listening to their micro lives in understanding infant care during the mid-twentieth century.

As the traveller who has once been from home is wiser than he who has never left his own doorstep, so a knowledge of one other culture should sharpen our ability to scrutinize more steadily, to appreciate more lovingly, our own. (Mead, 1928:1)

FIGURE 9.1 The cradle, Berthe Morisot (1872).

Alloparenting and the shadow mother

In contrast to the attachment-led practice often associated with infant care this chapter illuminates alternative views, introducing a wider lens to studying infant care. Cultural attitudes, beliefs and understandings of infant care include those who are delivering the caring role. In the previous chapters this has included the wet nurse, the nanny, the midwife, the nursery carer to name but a few. The term for this role is known as the 'shadow mother' or 'alloparenting', thought to be a product of feminist evolutionary anthropology. Hrdy (2009), an anthropologist, explored styles of mothering that challenged the dominant Western view and imagery of maternity. Hrdy drew attention to activities, practices and other relationships impacted on infant survival, including grandparenting care, with the collective effort of raising infants it takes a village to raise a child. This deviates from the exclusivity of primary carer and infant attachment theory of relationships. She focused on the importance of a range of caregivers beyond the biological mother, in their caring behaviours such as feeding and holding. 'Alloparenting' contributes another dimension to maternal bonding and the influence of others in their action and context (Knott, 2020). Social anthropology as a discipline considered provides a valuable starting point in developing the discussion around community care in other cultures and infant care beyond the West, specifically England (Knott, 2020).

Social anthropology

Social anthropology was often considered the study of other international lesser-known cultures. Initially in studying cultures anthropologists tended to evaluate stories and accounts from 'others' fieldwork, including those of travellers, missionaries or secondary sources such ancient texts. By the end of the twentieth century, in pursuit of studying communities and societies, anthropologists began to travel internationally and research for themselves. Today anthropologists continue to work internationally as well as locally. Anthropologists explore the social relationships of human beings in relation to their culture, including family structures, religion, political and economic life and how societies operate culturally (Lancy, 2014). A cultural view includes the processes and outcomes of societies with their set of values, customs and beliefs and practices, which constitutes a way of life for a specific group of people. This included studies about childhood, although this received more attention only during the twentieth century.

From an anthological perspective infancy can be viewed as a generational concept with a position in society, in relation to their mothers. Moreover, it fosters an understanding about patriarchal societies and societal value placed on maternal and infant care. Studying through an anthropological lens, place in space can matter alongside social geography and difference. A move away from binary dichotomies has been replaced with complimentary rather than conflicting discourses when discussing parents caring for their infants. In understanding these discourses anthropologists live the experiences and carry out observations and record discourses and practices known as ethnographical research (Kehily, 2013).

The word 'ethnography' comes from two Greek words: 'ethos' meaning people and 'graphia' meaning writing. This is helpful to know as it explains the anthropologists' attempt to interpret facts of social and cultural life.

Ethnography can be defined as both a research method and the outcome of the process in which anthropologists attempt to explain and interpret facts of social and cultural lives. However, it should be noted that it goes beyond simple descriptions or a list of facts. It attempts to describe and explain the life and culture of the group studied and takes an insider's perspective (Montgomery, 2009).

Contemplative case studies of care

Reading the following case studies provides an insight into alternative forms of infant care unfamiliar to those living in the West. They provide an opportunity to discuss the way we perceive and assume a specific and personal approach to care often considered as the 'appropriate way'.

Case Study 1: Margaret Mead's anthropological studies on Samoan children (1928)

This is a valuable illustration of living within a community, and whilst there has been criticism of the authenticity of Margaret Mead's evaluation, her work remains an important study in understanding about the life of communities. Important because it offers an insight beyond Western thinking and conceptualizations of infancy and care. Mead began her studies of Samoa and the South Pacific and viewed the difference between various people as culture rather than a biological lens, with the aim to analyse the daily lives of Samoan girls, from infancy through to early childhood and adolescence. By collecting data from observations and discussions with young women and girls she identified several cultural reasons why growing up there was less stressful to both the individual and society than in the United States. The lack of choices observed created more order and life revolved around the villages and their family. Marrying and having children were part of the life course, remaining in the communities until they died. They believed in one religion and attended church. There were no alternative belief systems operating. She wrote about the active part of the family rhythms of life and death. She included play among the children included caring for their infant siblings, relatives and friends. She observed their caring and playful approaches were reminiscent of how dolls were played with in the West. She noted infants were constructed by their abilities, development and growth and these were defined as:

- lap baby,
- knee baby,
- yard baby,
- community ages of childhood (LeVine and New, 2008:25).

Interestingly some of the yard infants desired to remain knee infants and their newfound independence was observed by Mead as challenging for the yard infants. They struggled in competing for female adult attention. Anthropologists have long been familiar with this account of the transition from infant to the toddler period as a stressful experience. This has also been recorded in the transition to and from the breast, with an increasing loss of close physical contact with mother. This was evaluated in Bali in 1938 in the treatment of infants as independent with greater social responsibility than the lap baby, often observed to show digressed behaviour, jealousy and teasing. It was evaluated these infants portrayed a sense of living in limbo. They were not quite old enough to go and be part of the independent older children in their community but perceived by their parents as too old to be treated as an infant with dependent needs (Kehily, 2013a).

Case Study 2: Living in a commune: The kibbutz

One of the first organized kibbutz was established in Israel during 1909, and by 1920 there were 1,800 members living in settlements. The figures increased with people residing in 224 settlements by the 1960s. After the First World War the first generation of settlers arrived in Israel and were committed to group ideals. These early pioneers rejected the patriarchal structures that were common in Eastern Europe, forming a new society with socialist and Zionist principles. The relevance from an anthropological perspective were how the infants were cared for. This was carried out through a collective approach in the kibbutz. Trained staff supervised the cleanliness and time keeping with socializations being an important part of the day. Food rationing was organized with women, and these were distributed equally to children. Separate clothes were also acquired centrally. Communal practice was favoured in raising family life with members elected to share a cooperative lifestyle (Spiro, 1975:143). Children in many kibbutz were raised from six months, and often earlier in communal 'children's houses', monitored at night by rotating shifts of night watchmen (and women), who, with the aid of an intercom system, were supposed to locate and respond to children's night-time needs.

Infant and young children experience of the kibbutz

Whilst many cultures internationally practise some form of communal child-rearing, the kibbutz is the only known society in history to attempt communal sleeping. Early kibbutzim gravitated towards the system for several reasons. Ideologically, kibbutz members wanted to break away from old Jewish-European traditions. They wanted to demolish the nuclear family structure in favour of the group. Members also wanted their infants to be raised in a microcosm of the kibbutz system, preparing them for their future lives. Economically, raising children collectively made sense, particularly when food was rationed. There was also a feminist motive, as communal sleeping was supposed to free women to participate equally in community life, and this contrasted with the existing patriarchal society members had lived in.

Most of the infants' and young children's time was spent in the children's house with peers. They ate, played, studied and slept there. They would visit parents every afternoon between 4pm and 8pm; then they would return to the children's house to sleep. Jewish mothers never cooked them a meal, never washed their clothes or sang a lullaby. The kibbutz system sought to limit private intimacies in case they diverted members' energy from the communal project.

The pressure to conform was considered relentless, with individuality and competition rejected within and among the members. Children who were unusual, eccentric or sought to distinguish themselves were shunned. They were socialized to be strong and positive in their outlook to life. Emotional expression was demeaned as weak and self-involved (Shpancer, 2019).

An anthropologist's evaluation of mother and infant care in a kibbutz

Individuals had to obtain permission to have an infant within a kibbutz, and during childbirth the tradition was for the mother to avoid shouting or crying during labour. A week after confinement the infant was often placed in a nursery. There were generally six baby cribs available at any one time and a playroom accommodating the infants. Swaddling was carried out, but loosely, and Sabbath clothes were worn. Interaction with the infants were by one trained and one untrained allocated member. Parents would visit in the evening and during the night watch checks were carried out by the allocated members. Observations were carried out by the birth mothers during the evening with their infants involved in a mix of feeding time as well as socializing among other women with their infants. There were few interactions observed with their infants, and mothers would often leave their infants after twenty minutes of carrying out their caring responsibilities. They would return to the nursery only if the infant was restless and had been called upon (Sagi et al., 1994).

In more recent times mothers in the kibbutz became more relaxed regarding hygiene and preparation time to feed. Peer groups were around communal feeding, and the mother could leave family worship if they needed to care for their infant (Spriro, 1975).

Connections with contemporary care practices

Salonen et al. (2020) carried out a study on evening early childhood care and education in Norway. As part of the study observations were used to understand the type of care received in nurseries that operated during a 24-hour period and late into the evening, to accommodate parent working arrangements. This form of care is expanding in the UK, with many nurseries opening from 6.00am to 8.00pm and increased settings opening throughout a 24-hour period (McAlees, 2016). It seems whilst the rationale has moved from community living to nuclear family groupings, unsociable employment hours and shift work are increasingly accepted with little financial alternatives. Consequently, group care, institutional settings, offering longer hours, are dependent on by parents in providing infant care, particularly with families who have little extended family support.

Contemplative question

Consider the following question from a professional and parental perspective.

What are the advantages and disadvantages to infant care when they are in settings at times beyond the 9.00am–5.00pm?

How is evening care delivered in settings and are there differences to day care?

Autobiographical research and infant care in the twentieth century

This latter part of the chapter invites the reader to consider an auto-/biographical perspective to the value of minutiae narratives and exploring infant care. In contrast to the ethnographical lens of community and culture this approach takes singular personal narrative in understanding how maternal and infant care was experienced. In the following three examples reflective narratives about infant care during the mid-twentieth century are explored.

Listening to mothers' narratives about their infant care from the mid-twentieth century has been a valuable journey and chimes with the themes and practices discussed in previous chapters. Biographical research compliments anthropological studies of observing actions, practices, beliefs and discourses. Biography focuses on the inner worlds of the individual, and their interpretations as they contextualize lived experiences. It uses various empirical sources, including life narratives, oral stories, documents, both official and personal, diaries, memorials, film and imagery (Larsen, 1992).

FIGURE 9.2 Captured everyday memories.

Through an in-depth analysis of sources, life history can be defined as a construction created by the participant, enabling an understanding about the categories, elaborations and personal theories they construct around their own lives (Goodson, 2001). Hence, autobiography is not only a methodological model for hermeneutic (an interpretation) understanding of individual lives, but also access to the complexity of social life from within (Denzin, 2008a).

Voices from the past

The following three narratives during the mid-twentieth century are reflective accounts of three women, unknown to each other and living in different parts of England. These included Hertfordshire, Devon and Dorset. They discussed what they deemed meaningful in evaluating their own experiences about infant care (Denzin, 2008b). The narratives draw parallels with Oakley's (1992) maternity and motherhood of the 1970s.

Viewed historically, in the 1960s Britain, women may have worked part-time if necessary, although they generally began when their children started school. Childminders were also used to help with the care-giving and paid employment, although there was often a sense of temporarily about the types of care used. Oral histories suggest that for some mothers' distinctive forms of organizational labour was employed, described by one woman as getting 'all these systems in place', to navigate the competing demands of family, home and workplace. Women managed and had knowledge of all the tasks needed to be carried out daily, including the predictable and unpredictable practicalities of domestic life (Goodson, 2001; Oakley, 1981b).

Parent–infant relations

In recent years Alison Gopnik (2017) has evaluated parenting from two domains: the carpenter and the gardener. Gopnik (2017) viewed the carpenter as the parent who has a preconceived idea of their child, framing upbringing by followed rules with less of a focus on individuality and resisting opportunity for any experimentation in their practice, preferring to teach skills. The 'gardener', by contrast, nurtures the child akin to a plant in a rich, varied environment, with personal growth supported. The infant and young child require 'a protected early period' when their needs are met unconditionally, with space for exploration and varied experiences. Diana Baumrind in the 1960s also described important dimensions of parenting. These were warmth (as opposed to conflict or neglect) and control strategies. Parenting typologies were, thus, constructed from a cross of warmth, conflict and control:

- authoritative (high warmth, positive and assertive control)
- authoritarian (low warmth and high conflict)
- permissive (high warmth but with low control attempts and expectations)
- neglectful (low warmth and control minimal).

These four typologies have been repeatedly associated with child outcomes. In Western society attachment leads the way between infant and carer in both personal and professional infant carer relationships. In exploring the following case studies parenting approaches to infant care are discussed alongside capturing the experiences of a mother's life during a time and place (McNamee, 2016).

Contemplative question

Consider the types of parents discussed.

Are models of parenting helpful in understanding approaches of infant care, and do these fluctuate in the first three years of development?

The three auto-/biographical narratives of parents

Contemplative case study 1

Life Narrative one: DOB unknown
Married: 1963

Personal upbringing

Being at a boarding school myself I was used to rules and regulations I have often said to my children I must have been very strict at times with you all, but they said it was good training as it seems to have rubbed off on them in different ways. I must admit we are a wonderful happy family and now I am on my own they are also loving towards me and spoil me like mad when they visit as often as they can.

While I was still working at a bank in Whitehall London, I fell pregnant with my first child a son Steven born in November 1964. Leaving the bank in July I knew I would not be going back as my husband and I believed a mother's place was in the home, looking after him and the family.

Fifteen months later my daughter Sally was born in February 1966 and in 1971 my daughter Janet was born in July 1971. It was only when the children were at school that I took up freelancing journalism but eventually I was a book dealer, mostly attending book fairs and antique fairs. I was a mother in the 1960s.

Pregnancy

I had to be induced for my first baby Steven as the hospital said I was overdue. I didn't agree, but it was arranged that I went into hospital on a Wednesday. The procedure took place the next day, followed by an enema. That was the worst part. Then the baby arrived the following morning. Labour took roughly 6 to 7 hours. I remember I had arrived on the Wednesday with a very bad cold, but the doctor joked don't worry your baby won't be born with a cold, but he did have a lot of mucus which had to be removed through tubes. He weighed 6 pounds 12 ounces and I breastfed for the first few months or so. I did have gas and air at the time of the birth.

It was considered in the 1960s that if your previous birth had no complications you had your next baby at home. Therefore, I attended the antenatal clinic at my doctor's surgery and was introduced to my midwife. The day I was due, she came in the morning and made me drink a small glass of cod liver oil, followed by a piece of dry bread to keep it down. While cooking my husband's dinner in the evening I needed to call the midwife. When she arrived, she made me walk around the bed practically till the last moments. No gas or air this time and when my daughter Sally was born, she arrived crying. Apparently, that was not unusual, so she told me. My husband came upstairs to see the baby, but I could tell he was disappointed it wasn't another boy. I knew he was hoping to have all boys. It did upset me at the time but in later life he seemed to be closer to the girls than his son although he was very proud of his achievements getting to a top University and leaving with a science degree and having a very successful, high position in a publishing company. Sally weighed 7 pounds 6 ounces and I breast fed her for just a few months. My doctor came the following day as I needed stitches.

Five years later an unplanned birth but very welcomed was the birth of my daughter Janet. The first signs were at 3:00 am on Saturday morning. My husband drove me to the hospital and she arrived eventually at 3:00 pm. The duty doctor gave me an epidural injection in my spine, then the rest was done by forceps. Janet, my daughter weighed 7 pounds 15 ounces and I breast fed her but not as long as the other babies. I must admit I cannot remember a lot of advice coming from the doctor or nurses that wasn't common sense. I think the best advise came from my mother-in-law you who told me you must have a routine.

A routine was not only for feeding times but especially with potty training, which was successful. I was very lucky to have her around when I needed her. My own mother would have wanted to dictate and practically take over, whereas my mother-in-law was very understanding and a real treasure. I never had to use childminders as they do today. I attended evening classes for handicrafts and dress making but had to eventually give them up as Janet, my daughter was a handful at the best of times. She was very strong minded and seemed to know when I was not around. She would kick up such a fuss. Again, my husband was no good when they were babies but great when they got nearer to school age. I needed a car, especially for ferrying the children to different schools. These were shared with other mothers and was a great help if their cars would not start on cold frosty mornings.

Before my two eldest children started school, they attended a nursery school at the age of four just mornings however I made a big mistake by not sending my younger when the time came. I thought having a brother and sister it would not be necessary as they were already teaching her to tell the time and counting numbers. Unfortunately, when she started her first school, she felt very disadvantaged especially in the cloakroom and about asking to go to the toilet it made me feel very guilty for a long time.

Preparing for Parenthood

I knew my husband was not going to be a hands-on father like my own father. He believed that the house shopping and looking after the children was my department. Therefore, he was not involved in nappy changing or bath time.

He was never home in time or there to read them a bedtime story. Although this sounds very selfish on his part, he did work long hours leaving home for London at 8:00am and was not usually home until 8.00pm. However, I was never short of money for myself or the children, whatever we needed he was more than generous.

My mother-in-law was a great help, especially when she came to live with us in her granny flat that we had built over a double garage. She would do all my mending and ironing but I did all the cooking. She did help with preparations in the kitchen, so we worked together for a short time. Then we both decided we need a cleaner once a week. I still think the most important thing regarding bringing up children is routine, not only when they are babies but later on regarding bedtimes and restriction on sweets and biscuits.

This snapshot depicted community life and family caring responsibilities, with clearly established roles between the mother, father and mother-in-law. It provided a description about responsibilities and daily routines of caring for three infants. The experience of childbirth-linked home life with hospital and the communication of professionals was considered common sense and the generational advice more valuable. Verbal communication about care was evident.

Contemplative case study 2

Life Narrative two: 09.08.1947

I had two babies, the first in 1966 and the second in 1967, with 11 months between them.

Pregnancy

The first pregnancy was a surprise because I did not think I could get pregnant so quickly. We had a certain amount of sex education at school, but that was it. So, I bought a baby book that was popular at the time, Dr Spock's. I read it from cover to cover and thought I would be fine. I had a trouble free pregnancy. I went to my doctor for monthly checks of water and blood pressure – but no 16 week scans ever, so we did not know the sex of the baby beforehand.

I went full term and the baby was two weeks late. I started having pains at 5.00 am in the morning and had a police escort to a hospital in London (my husband was in the Met at the time). I entered the ward where six mothers were also in bed at various stages. Some were louder than others and there was not a lot of privacy on the ward. I was given a bath and a shave and an enema, which I found most uncomfortable. I was put into bed and waited. The pain became worse, so they gave me an epidural. I became sleepy and did not realise I was ready to push, until they rushed me into the delivery room. By then, husbands were allowed in. My husband, being a farmer's son, thought it would be like a cow calving – easy! I was in labour for 12 hours, which at the time was traumatic for a 19 year old. My first daughter was born weighing 9lb 2oz. I received a few stiches and was washed down and put into bed. The baby was taken and put into the nursery.

Motherhood

I was in hospital for a week. I came home with the new baby and tried breast feeding. No follow-up of a mid-wife visit, never mind any other midwife visits were carried out. No baby clinics were available so for any advice, I looked up Dr Spock, or I had a good friend who advised me. My milk dried up and I didn't realise it, so the baby went hungry and cried a lot. I went to the doctor who told me what had happened, so I went home and made up formula and she drank two bottles straight down.

I found motherhood okay, although I hated taking her for her injections. She was a good baby who started to walk at 10 months and began saying words at 12 months! Challenges were the worry of whether I was doing all the right things. I never went to work and lived in police flats in London where most families were coping with babies and young children and we exchanged ideas together. I found I was the youngest. She was a happy baby. She ate well and enjoyed company. She was restless at bedtime and liked a lot of cuddles. She had dolls and teddys but loved her books.

My second baby was a very different set of affairs. The first baby was only two months old when I found I was pregnant again. What a shock! I did not have a period between the first birth and being pregnant and did not think I could get pregnant again so quick. Coping with a baby and carrying a baby, I felt even more tired. The doctor said it was too quick after the first baby and I went for check-ups every month.

I decided to have the baby at home. Because the first baby had been overdue, they didn't want the same thing to happen again. We were all prepared for the due date and the midwife arrived and gave me something to move things along. It didn't work and she went home. When she came back later, the baby suddenly felt like she was jumping in my tummy, so I was taken into hospital, a London Hospital. They decided to induce, but nothing happened. They let me have a rest and the next day at 10 o'clock they gave me a saline drip to start the contractions, which worked. I was in labour for three hours, but she was only 5lb 4oz when she was born – tiny. She was taken away and put in an incubator. Thankful it was over, the experience left an impression on me that lasted until even now, in my 70s.

When the doctor came to see me afterwards, he accused me of smoking and that was why she was born so small. I have never smoked in my life. It turned out that our doctor had made a mistake in calculating the actual date and she'd been induced two months early. The police wanted to take the matter further, but I said no as we were both okay.

I came home and coping with a 12-month-old and a new baby was not easy. They wanted to keep me in hospital, but I asked to come home because it was the first baby's birthday. I had trouble feeding the new baby. It took ages to feed her and then she would burp and bring it all up and I'd have to start again. I couldn't breast feed her because the shock of her induced early delivery meant I didn't have any milk. Our doctor apologised for his mistake and if the babies were ever ill, he was straight on our doorstep.

Generational reflections

There are just a few things my mother told me when she was pregnant with me. I was born in 1947 and they paid for a doctor and a midwife. I was very late – about three weeks, which would not happen today. It was a bad delivery, and I was 10lb 4oz. My poor mother had to stay in bed for three weeks to recover. She was very reluctant to have another child, but she did and found it hard to bond with the baby after such a traumatic first birth.

This account revealed the lack of communication with health professionals and the reliance on popular parenting books of the time, this was Dr Spock. It also revealed how the experience of childbirth can have a long-lasting emotional impact and birth trauma can potentially affect bonding and attachment towards their infants. This was comparable with Llewellyn Davis Maternity Letters about maternity care.

Contemplative case study 3

Life Narrative Three: 14.03.1949

Conception

Planning a family was not really a thought. I believed I felt a maternal pull to be a mother. My friends were the same and although we were all about seventeen or eighteen we felt once we had met someone this was the normal thing to do next and was what I wanted.

Sex and families were not openly discussed, and I know there were homes for girls that had baby's underage (under 16 years) to help them look after their babies. All the babies were often given up for adoption. There was little sex education and sex and babies still did not seem to be related so there was

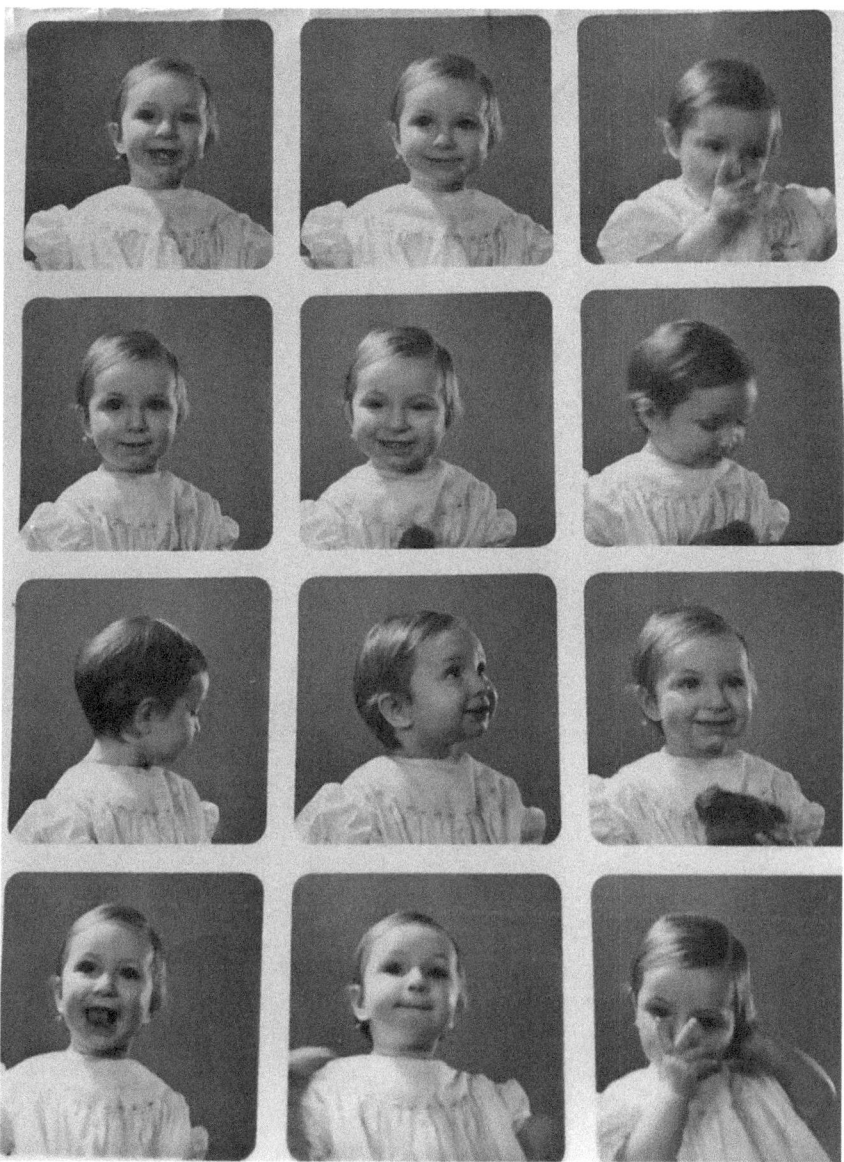

FIGURE 9.3 My experiences as a mother in the 1960s.

a lot I didn't really understand. I do remember my mother telling me when I was married that contraception was difficult as there was not any plastic and no pill. She did tell me what they did and I had a baby book. It was very different in those days and no one was really interested in your pregnancy until you were at least six months pregnant.

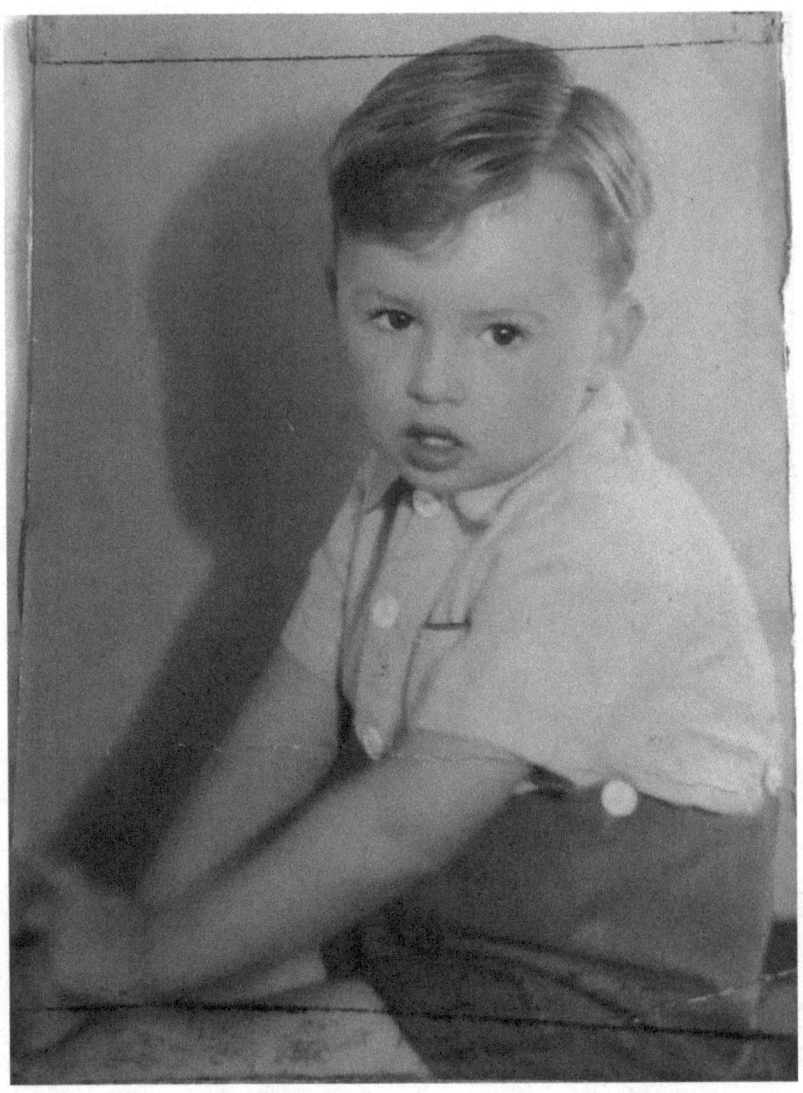

FIGURE 9.4 A personal lens.

The domestic home

I thought that I was very lucky when I had my first child, we had a nice flat that we rented from the lady who owned it. She lived downstairs and could not walk so we had the upper floor flat. I had my own furniture and so did not have to borrow anything. My parents and my husband's parents helped us with furniture too. I would make all the curtains and lamp shades and enjoyed doing things for the home to make it look nice. I enjoyed this lifestyle, making changes to the home with soft furnishings that I made. I would make drawstring bags for different items and I think I was very good at managing money for food and household things.

Birth experiences

My local family health clinic was within walking distance and I could walk there before I had the baby. I also had exercise classes and baby care classes. Husbands were encouraged to attend but with their work that was difficult. Husbands were not really encouraged at the birth and my husband was not present for my two home births. He was nearby but it was not normal to have him in the room with me, well not for me anyway.

The hospital visits were not a great experience and there was lots of queuing in draughty corridors to see people and being spoken over. During the first visits if you were not married you were made to feel embarrassed. They would check the weekly growth of the baby and their heartbeat.

My hospital birth was an induced labour and they cut and stitched me up again. I was not talked to, rather about and spoken over. I was given gas and air and must have had an injection as strips were used. A doctor was called I can't remember what the procedure is called. I was in hospital with my baby for a week. The other mothers were really helpful with advice. The staff sister did her rounds and made comments. The nurses were distant but attentive.

My parents didn't give me much advice as I had a boy and they were used to having a girl, me! I was brought a pram though and my cousins' wife was more helpful with feeding etc she was a baby foster carer. I found the health visit to not be very helpful although I continued to use the clinic. My doctor was probably the most helpful as a family doctor and knew the family ideas and us really well.

I had children born in the 1970s and 1980s and I have seen many changes. I think the support was much better in the 1960s and the 1970s. The health visitor was friendly but firm and the doctor and health visitor were helpful with advice. I was told I had to do things in a certain way with my first child and this has stayed with me. I was worried I would get things wrong so I followed their advice. I would also be told off if I hadn't done what they said. I wasn't very old so glad to listen and do what was told of me. There were no mobiles so I would have to go to the telephone box down the road, with a sick baby for any advice if I needed it.

Generational story

My mother was a teacher and went back to work when I was about one years old. The nursery that I went to was attached to the school she worked in. I have some photos of me there and it was very much outdoor play. I have a picture of myself playing in a sandbox. The staff in uniform looked rather like nurses of the time. In 1949 to 1950 I remember mum saying that she did not have any help when she had me and her mother worked, and her dad had a sub post office so she managed on her own. I think mum's sister-in-law was helpful as she had sisters so got advice from her. She was also three years older, and her daughter was three years older than me and live nearby, so it helped.

If you look at historical perspectives, you can find out from your past what affects your experiences has had on your behaviour and the way you think. I was told to have a routine and it was good but now I think it is much better for babies to have lots of cuddles.

We have many different family dynamics now, so it is important to envelope both parents and siblings together and develop the family structure from this. I felt when I was younger, I was not confident and felt I had to do what I was told. Now I would have more of a discussion, and I think this is important.

This account revealed the domestic space as being a caring and a homely environment in preparation for the infant birth and subsequent family life. Professional care seemed to be at arm's length and advice was followed rather than discussed during the perinatal stage. Prior to six months of pregnancy there was deemed little support and conception remained an elusive topic, not openly questioned by young adults.

Voices heard from the past

The three voices reflected on their experiences about infant care. The thread between them appeared to be the solidarity of women in similar circumstances and the power of a shared community in seeking support through the transition to parenthood. This was accessed through their extended family, women on the ward and groups at clinics post birth. The intention of including the voices was for the reader to reflect and connect with some of the topics discussed and linking to contemporary practices. The narratives provided an opportunity of the inner world of the mother and their positionality within their family dynamic. The domestic habitat is also mentioned alongside roles and the process of preparing the construction of family life, with the prime responsibility about caring for their infant(s). It also provided a wider social cultural understanding of the cultural lives of women during the mid-twentieth century and contextualized their choices in preparation for motherhood such as employment and domesticity.

Connections with contemporary care practices

The micro case studies contextualized the mother's maternal role and position in the family and society. The narratives presented an appreciation to the cultural landscape of Britain during this time. In understanding women's position in relation to mothering and working more broadly, sociologist Viola Klein embarked on a major investigation into the careers of married female graduates in Britain, during 1963. Klein's aim was to map patterns of paid work over the life-course and identify the determinants of women's movements in and out of the labour market, as they related to maternal care and child-rearing during the 1960s (McCarthy, 2020b). In analysing the questionnaires McCarthy revealed the longer-term impact and opportunities, including the lack of them when having a family young and the expectations of returning to employment later in life during the mid-twentieth century. The studies' biographical findings highlighted the gratification women felt when they had invested in training and wanted to continue pursuing their career alongside having a family. This contrasted with the three narratives included whereby their aim had been to secure their position as primary carer and mother in the domestic home, although they too had reflected on their previous and return to paid work. This emphasizes their changing identities transitioning from a woman to mother. It underscores the diverse roles women embark on when becoming a parent and their position and contribution within the family dynamic. Today the discourse about parenthood and employment continues. For many mothers the pursuit of employment, caring for their infants, work at home and accessing childcare beyond family members remain an emotional, financial and identity tension. The reality in England is that financially many mothers continue to work paid part-time work. Although this seems an acceptable resolution in reducing possible internal feelings alloparenting it can also be perceived to add a further constraint to successfully caring or wanting to exclusively care for their infant.

Conclusion: A personal note

Including original narratives was an aspect that complimented the anthropological studies from the past. It highlighted the value of micro voices and how individual stories can aid a deep understanding into history. Rather than making broad generalizations about periods of history, which was not the intension, it captured the lived experiences of those from the past. The narratives can therefore invite a comparison and broader readings about lives in a particular period in history. It therefore provides the how and why of choices and restrictions, the micro stories of caring for infants.

Conclusion: Looking back, moving forward

The research and writing of historical perspectives on infant care has been an emotional labour, with the privilege to have had the opportunity to explore the topics as an academic and mother of four. Through studying topics about infant care from books, as well as attending professional and academic conferences, virtual webinars and meetings I have been able to reflect on the wider landscape of infant care.

I have also reflected on the past year during the pandemic, living within a community where we have had to socially distance, lock down and then resume partially back into society. This has limited physical geographical movements, missing those close to us under the veil of a potentially life-threatening contagious virus. A scenario perhaps familiar to those previously lived generations. As an alternative form of communication, accessing the internet has ensued in existing part-time, through a virtual world. This has led me to reflect on the past and present. Whilst the world from a Western professional woman feels more accessible, albeit virtually, even during the pandemic, it is a stark reminder of the dependence with technology, the resources, knowledge and finances privileged with. The reduction of physical contact, and ways of sustaining communication, including mothers with limited access to technology, has often culminated in an isolated and restricted experience. Parenthood is an immense personal transitional period and makes me think about the way women have recently sought a space for these important discussions. Do women predominantly draw on parenting advice from media in relating and listening to those with a public image and brand to identify with how they are feeling or what they should do? Alternatively, do they seek and follow advice from the professional, authoritarian voice?

Reports such as *The Babies in Lockdown Report* (2020) have drawn attention to the financial challenges and mental health new mothers have experienced during the pandemic. They also include ways of moving forward, regarding policy changes, professional support and services available. This resonated with my readings of mothers from the past such as *The Maternity Letters* Margaret Llewelyn Davies collated as a way of seeking policy change and highlighting the daily challenges new mothers faced in caring for their infants during the early twentieth century. Similarly, *The Mass Observation* diaries have been used numerous times as a way of highlighting individual circumstances and how mothers have cared for their infant and home during post-war England. Further biographies from other sources including Burnett, Rowbotham and Bland within the chapters also provide further voices to understanding infant care.

This last year has also meant slowing down and relying on those close to us, overcoming maternal challenges unforeseen for many in recent years. This includes re-shifting childcare arrangements, relying on alternative transportation, challenges to accessing professionals, health and social care. Finances have also been impacted because of the pandemic, with many families secure and established employment lost. This has resulted in changing occupations, and for many relying on community foodbanks to feed their family, in the short- and long-term future. The everyday experiences of today remind me of family life in the past and have given me time to savour and appreciate my role as academic and mother. I have renewed reflections about how the past influences the present and will inform our future. By predominately researching mothers there is an argument that it somehow reduces the father's role and certainly this was not a deliberate intentional drive of the book. As Knott (2020) highlighted in her research there is an argument that in exclusively discussing the mother and infant dynamic there is a risk of confirming their position in society as a separate sphere, and compounding the female, male positions in society. However, the prominent discourses in history have often been in favour of male writers and male accounts of pregnancy, childbirth and infant care. This book adds to the literature, within the realms of gender inclusivity about how women as mothers support infant care and historically this role has often, although not exclusively, been assigned to women, with an agreement that mothering can be carried out by fathers too.

The book also discussed the role of alloparenting and the shadow mother, within education, and institutional history therefore not exclusively undertaken by the biological mother. Foundling hospitals, workhouses, formalized day care have all acted in loco parentis to varying degrees, and these have been included in broadening the discussions around infant care. Furthermore, women regarded as mother figures or replacement mothers including wet nursers, dames and nannies have also been included to reflect on the roles and activities of infant care.

As a starting position to this book, I wanted to explore some shifting concepts about infant care. My initial readings were from, David Morgan's (1996) definition of family in what they 'do' rather than what they 'are' and Sarah Knott's (2019) discussion of mother as a verb. It therefore seems appropriate to close with the following terms

- infant and mother as the identity of the individual
- infanthood and motherhood as a discourse, an ideology and institution, with their characterizations having dominated historical accounts of maternity.

In weaving these two terms together I considered the themes introduced and discussed in the book will ignite further interest and research with readers, offering specific areas to pursue in the future.

REFERENCES

Ainsworth, M. (1979a). Infant–mother attachment. *American Psychologist*. 34(10): 932–7.

Ainsworth, M. (1979b). The effects of maternal deprivation: A review of findings and controversy in the context of research strategy. In M. D. Ainsworth and R. G. Andry (Eds.), *Deprivation of maternal care*. Geneva: World Health Organization. 97–165.

Allen, C. (2016). In the 50 years since Cathy come home things have got much worse. In https://www.theguardian.com/society/2016/jul/31/cathy-come-home-50-years-homelessness-mental-health-problems. Accessed 28/10/2019.

Anderson, M. (2007). *Approaches to the history of the western family 1500 to 1914*. Cambridge: Cambridge University Press.

Anderson, M. (2013). 19th century childbirth. In https://adelaidia.history.sa.gov.au/subjects/19th-century-childbirth. Accessed 15/08/2020.

Anderson-Faithful, S. (2018). *Mary Sumner*. Cambridge: Lutterworth Press.

Andrews, H. (1909). *Midwifery for nurses*. London: Edward Arnold.

Aries, P. (1962). *Centuries of childhood a social history of family life*. London: Vintage Books.

Athan, A. and L. Miller. (2005). Spiritual awakening through the motherhood journey. *Journal of the Motherhood Initiative for Research and Community Involvement*. 7(1): 17–31.

Atkinson, C. (2005). *The monument of matrones* Volume 3 (Lamps 5–7) essential works for the study of early modern women, Series III. Part One, Volume 6. London: Routledge.

Atkinson, C. and J. B. Atkinson (1991). Subordinating women: Thomas Bentley's use of biblical women in *the monument of matrones* (1582). Church history. 289–300.

Aztec Cradleboard Figurine and Drawing [Object], in Children and Youth in History, Item #432. In https://chnm.gmu.edu/cyh/items/show/432. Accessed 30/01/2021.

Badcock, C. (2000). *Evolutionary psychology: A critical introduction*. Cambridge (UK): Polity Press.

Bakhtin, M. (1981). *The dialogic imagination*. Austin: University of Texas.

Bakwin, H. (1942). Loneliness in infants. *Am J Dis Child*. 63(1): 30–40. doi:10.1001/archpedi.1942.02010010031003. In https://jamanetwork.com/journals/jamapediatrics/article-abstract/1179366. Accessed 17/10/2019.

Barlow, J. (2018) in P. Leach. *Transforming infant well-being: Research policy and practice for the first 1001 critical days*. London: Routledge. 53.

Barnes, P. (1995). *Personal, social and emotional development of children*. Milton Keynes: Blackwell Publishing.

Barrett, H. (1875). *The management of infancy and childhood in health and disease*. London: George Routledge.

Baxter, S. (2011). Too much too young children of the middle ages. In *https://www.bbc. co.uk/programmes/b013rknh*. Accessed 29/10/2018.

Berry, H. (2019). *Orphans of the empire*. Oxford: Oxford University Press.

Bhullar, I. (2016). Beatrice Webb, Clara Collet and Charles Booth's survey of London. In https://blogs.lse.ac.uk/lsehistory/2016/03/21/potter-collet-booth/. Accessed 05/08/2020.

Bigner, R. K. and J. J. Yang (1996). Parent education in popular literature: 1972-1990. *Family & Consumer Sciences Research Journal*. 25(1): 3–27.

Bland, L. (2019). *Britain's brown babies*. Manchester: Manchester University Press.

Blow, S. (1985[1895]). *The song I music or Frederick Froebel my mother play*. London: Appleton and Company.

Bolzman, L. (2009). The advent of child rights on the international scene and the role of the save the children. *International Union* 1920–45 (Refugee Survey Quarterly. 27(4). Doi:10.1093/rsq/hdn053https://core.ac.uk/download/pdf/85211503.pdf.

Bower, M. and J. Trowell (2002). *The emotional needs of young children and their families: Using psychoanalytic ideas in the community*. London: Routledge.

Bowlby, J. (1969). *Attachment: Attachment and loss: Vol. 1. Loss*. New York: Basic Books.

Boyd, W. (1956). *Émile for today: The Émile of Jean Jacques Rousseau selected, translated and interpreted by William Boyd*. London: Heinemann.

Brody, S. (1967). *Mother-infant interaction [Film]*. Washington, DC: National Library of Medicine.

Bronfenbrenner, U. (1979). *The ecology of human development*. Cambridge: Harvard University Press.

Brough, J., M. Dionne, A. Dionne, C. Dionne and Y., Dionne (1965). '*We were five': The Dionne quintuplets' story from birth through girlhood to womanhood*. New York: Simon and Schuster.

Bruce, T (2021). *Friedrich froebel*. London: Bloomsbury Academic.

Burnett, J. (1984). *Useful toil*. London: Penguin.

Burnett, J. (1985). *Destiny obscure*. London: Penguin.

Bynum, W. (2002). Childless father of Eugenics. *Science*. 296(5567). In https://science.sciencemag.org/content/296/5567/472?hwoasp=authn%3A1589555689%3A256%3A2954608812%3A0%3A0%3AIhtBZvtabyhCEdPL5ORZHw%3D%3D. Accessed 05/08/2020.

Cadogan, W. (1749). *An essay upon nursing, and the management of children from their birth to three years of age*. London: J. Roberts.

Carter, K. and Codell (2012). *The decline of therapeutic bloodletting and the collapse of traditional medicine*. New Brunswick and London: Transaction Publishers. ISBN 978-1-4128-4604-2.

Celebi, M. (2017). *Weaving the cradle*. London: Kingsley.

Chamberlain, G. (2006). British maternal mortality in the 19th and early 20th centuries. *Journal of the Royal Society of Medicine*. 99(11): 559–63. https://doi.org/10.1258/jrsm.99.11.559 https://www.ncbi.nlm.nih.gov/pmc/articles/PMC1633559/

Chamot, M., D. Farr and M. Butlin (1964). *Tate gallery: The modern British paintings, drawings and sculpture*. London: Aldbourne Press.

Christensson, K. (1998). Randomised study of skin to skin contact versus incubator care for rewarming low risk hypothermic neonates. *Lancet*. 352: 115.

Cohen, J. (2018). *A brief history of bloodletting*. In https://www.history.com/news/a-brief-history-of-bloodletting#:~:text=Considered%20one%20of%20medicine's%20oldest,overabundance%20of%20blood%2C%20or%20plethora. Accessed 23/12/2020.

Cohen, L. and S. Waite-Shipansky (2017). *Theories of early childhood and education*. London: Routledge.

Cohen, R. (2020). *Margaret Llewellyn Davis*. Dagenham: Merlin Press.

Cohen, S. (nd). 'Emile [Literary Excerpt].' In Children and Youth in History, Item #216, https://chnm.gmu.edu/cyh/items/show/216. Accessed 30/01/2021.

Coles, P. (2015). *The shadow of the second mother*. London: Routledge.

Connelln (2018). Jonas Hanway. In https://hist235.hist.sites.carleton.edu/timeline/jonas-hanway/. Accessed 28/10/2109.

Coram Adoption (nd). Adopting a baby: Early permanence. In https://www.coramadoption.org.uk/adoption-process/children-waiting-adoption/adopting-baby-early-permanence. Accessed 19/11/2019.

Coram Charity (2021). Coram Story. In https://coramstory.org.uk/corams-history/. Accessed 30/10/2019.

Cowan, J. (2021). *The secret life of Dorothy Soames: A foundling story*. London: Virago.

Crowe, B. (2013). *The playgroup movement*. United Kingdom: Taylor and Francis.

Crowther, S. and J. Hall (2018). *Spirituality and childbirth*. London: Routledge.

Culpepper, N. (1654). Culpeper's directory for midwives. Discovering, 1. The diseases in the privities of women. 2. The diseases of the privie part. 3. The diseases of the womb … 14. The diseases and symptoms in children. Culpeper, Nicholas, 1616-1654. In https://quod.lib.umich.edu/e/eebo/A69832.0001.001/1:1?rgn=div1;view=fulltext. Accessed 25/06/2020.

Cunningham, C. (2006). *The invention of childhood*. London: BBC Books.

Cunningham, H. (2017). *Children and childhood in western society since 1500*. London: Pearson Education limited.

Cushman, P. (1995). *Constructing the self, constructing America: A cultural history of psychotherapy*. Cambridge, MA: Perseus.

Darwin, C. (2009[1872]). *The expression of the emotions in man and animals*. London: Penguin.

Davies, M. (1904). *The women's co-operative guild 1883 to 1904*. Westmoreland: Women's Co-Operative Guild.

Davies, M. (1978a). *Maternity letters from working women*. London: Virago Press.

Davies, M. (1978b). *No one but a woman knows*. London: Virago Press.

Davies, M. (2012). *Life as we have known it*. London: Virago Press.

Davis, A. (2014). *Modern motherhood*. Manchester: Manchester Press.

Dawson, D. and K. W. Fischer (Eds.) (1994). *Human behavior and the developing brain*. New York: Guilford Press.

DeCasper, J. and W. Fifer (1980). Human bonding; new-borns prefer their mothers' voices. *Science*. 208(4448): 1174–6.

Degtardi, S. and B. Davis (2008). Understanding infants: Characteristics of early childhood practitioners' interpretations of infants and their behaviours. *Early Years*. 28(3): 221–34.

DeLoache, J. S. and A. Gottlieb (2000). *A world of babies: Imagined childcare guides for seven societies.* Cambridge: Cambridge University Press. https://doi.org/10.1017/CBO9780511818004

Denzin, N. and Y. Lincoln (Eds.) (2008a). *Handbook of qualitative research.* Thousand Oaks, CA: Sage.

Denzin, N. and Y. Lincoln (2008b). *Collecting and interpreting qualitative materials.* London: Sage.

Derricourt, R. (2018). *Unearthing childhood.* Manchester: Manchester University Press.

Devore, I. and M. J. Konner (2019). Infancy in hunter-gatherer life: An ethological perspective. In Norman F. White (Ed.), *Ethology and Psychiatry.* Toronto: University of Toronto Press. 113–41. https://doi.org/10.3138/9781487575663-009

Dickens, C. [1844] (2008). *A christmas carol.* Oxford: Oxford University Press.

Douglass, S. (nd). Earthenware mold of a swaddled child [object] in Children and Youth in History, Item #215. In https://chnm.gmu.edu/cyh/items/show/215. Accessed 30/01/2021.

Douglass, S. (nd). Sippy Cup [Artifact/Object] in Children and Youth in History, Item #220. In https://chnm.gmu.edu/cyh/items/show/220. Accessed 30/01/2021.

Drife, J. (2002). The start of life: A history of obstetrics. *Postgraduate Medical Journal.* 78: 311–5.

Dryden, L., R. Forbes, P. Mukherji and L. Pound (2005). *Essential early years.* London: Hodder Arnold.

Dunn, P. (2000). Dr William Buchan (1729–1805) and his domestic medicine archives of disease in childhood. *Fetal and Neonatal Edition* 83: F71-F73. In https://fn.bmj.com/content/83/1/F71.info. Accessed 22/02/2019.

Dunn, P. M. (1999). The Chamberlen family (1560–1728) and obstetric forceps. Archives of Disease. *Childhood Fetal and Neonatal Edition.* 81: F232–F234. In https://fn.bmj.com/content/81/3/F232 Accessed 06/08/2020.

Dutton, R. (1969). *Rousseau, Jean-Jacques. Emile.* New York: E.P.

Ehrenreich, B. (2010). *Witches, midwives, and nurses* (2nd ed.): *A history of women healers.* CUNY: The Feminist Press.

Ekirch, A. R. (2001). Sleep we have lost: Pre-industrial slumber in the British Isles. *American Historical Review.* 106(2): 343–86.

Elfer, P., E. Goldschmied and D., Selleck (2011). *Key persons in the nursery building relationships for quality provision.* London: David Fulton Books.

Engel, G. L. (1980). The clinical application of the biopsychosocial model. *American Journal of Psychiatry.* 137: 535–44. In https://doi.org/10.1176/ajp.137.5.535.

Evans, B. (2013). How autism became autism: The radical transformation of a central concept of child development in Britain. *History of the Human Sciences.* 26(3): 3–31.

Finnegan, F. and Drake, M. (Eds) (1994). *From family tree to family history* (studying family and community history, Series Number 1). London: Cambridge University Press.

Forster, M. (2003). *Diary of an ordinary women.* London: Chatto and Windus.

Fraiberg, S. (2019) in J. Raphael-Leff (2019) *Parent-Infant psychodynamics: Wild things, mirrors and ghosts* (1st ed.). London: Routledge. https://doi.org/10.4324/9780429478154

Freeman, H. (2016). Attachment parenting: The best way to raise a child – or maternal masochism? In https://www.theguardian.com/lifeandstyle/2016/jul/30/

attachment-parenting-best-way-raise-child-or-maternal-masochism. Accessed 02/11/2020.

Froebel, F. (1920). *Mother's songs, games, and stories*. London: William Rice.

Fulton, J. F. (1950). *Logan clendening lectures on the history and philosophy of medicine*. Kansas: University of Kansas Press.

Galton, F. (1874). *English men of science: Their nature and nurture*. London: Routledge.

Gathorne-Hardy, J. (1973). *The rise and fall of the British Nanny*. London: Victorian book club.

Gershon, L. (2015). The lifesaving, horrifying history of wet nurses. In https://daily. jstor.org/lifesaving-horrifying-history-wet-nurses/ Accessed 05/11/2020.

Gesell, A. (1943). *Infant* and *child care in the culture of today*. UK: Read Books.

Goldschmied, E. and S. Jackson (2004). *People under three, young children in day care*. (2nd ed.) London: Routledge.

Goodall, M. (2020). Humanist heritage: Unearthing the rich history of humanism in the UK with Madeleine Goodall. In https://humanism.org.uk/2020/03/30/ humanist-heritage-unearthing-the-rich-history-of-humanism-in-the-uk-with-madeleine-goodall/. Accessed 02/03/2021.

Goodson, I. (2001). *Life history research in educational settings: Learning from lives (doing qualitative research in educational settings*. Open University Press: Milton Keynes.

Goodwin, W. (2018). Age old practice of wet/cross nursing. leLeche league UK. In http://www.prweb.com/releases/2008/09/prweb1352564.htm. Accessed 05/11/2020.

Gopnik, A. (2017). *The gardener and the carpenter: What the new science of child development tells us about the relationship between parents and children*. England: Vintage.

Gordon, O. (2019). *The first breath*. London: Bluebird Books.

Graham, H. (1950). *Eternal eve*. London: William Heinemann Medical Books Ltd,

Grant, J. (1998). *Raising baby by the book: The education of American mothers*. New Haven, CT: Yale University Press.

Greanleaf, B. K. (1978). *Children through the ages: A history of childhood*. New York: McGraw-Hill. 64–7.

Grieco, S. F. and C. A. Corstini (1991). *Historical perspectives on breastfeeding*. Italy: UNICEF.

Halliday, J. (1948) in R. Hayward (2009). Enduring emotions: James L. Halliday and the Invention of the psychosocial. *Isis Journal*. 100(4): 827–38.

Harde, R. (2002). What was your living mother's mind? Motherhood as intellectual enterprise in Mother's legacy books. *Journal of the Association for Research on Mothering*. 4(3). In file:///C:/Users/Amanda.Norman/Downloads/ Whatwasyourlivingmothersmind%20(1).pdf.

Hardyment, C. (2007). *Dream babies*. London: Francis Lincoln.

Harlow (1950) in J. Bowlby (1969). *Attachment: Attachment and loss: Vol. 1. Loss*. New York: Basic Books.

Harries, V. and A. Brown (2017). The association between use of infant parenting books that promote strict routines, and maternal depression, self-efficacy, and parenting confidence. *Early Child Development and Care*. 1–12. http:// onlinelibrary.wiley.com/doi/10.1002/imhj.20071/pdf

Hartley, L. P. (1953) in L. P. Hartley (2004). *The go-between*. London: Penguin Classics. 1.

Hays, J. (2015). Children in India. In http://factsanddetails.com/india/People_and_Life/sub7_3d/entry-4178.html. Accessed 02/05/2019.

Hayward, R (2009). Enduring emotions: James L. Halliday and the invention of the psychosocial. *Isis Journal*. 100(4): 827–38.

Hearn, K. (2020). *Portraying pregnancy*. London: Paul Holberton Publishing.

Heller, J. (2016). *The mother's legacy in early modern England*. London: Routledge.

Hendrick, H. (1997a). *Child welfare England 1872 to 1989*. London:Routledge.

Hendrik, H. (1997b). *Children chartered an English society 1880 to 1990*. Cambridge: Cambridge University Press.

Hewitt, M. (1999). District visiting and the constitution of domestic space in the Mid-Nineteenth century. In I. Bryden and J. Floyd (Eds.), *Domestic space: Reading the nineteenth-Century interior*. Manchester: Manchester University Press. 121–41.

Heywood, C. (2017). *A history of childhood*. Cambridge: Polity Press.

Higginbotham, P. (2017). *Children's homes: An institution of care for Britain's young*. Barnsley: Pen and Sword.

Higginson, J. (1974). Dame schools. *British Journal of Educational Studies*. 22(2): 166–81. Doi:10.2307/3119841

Hobbes, T. (1600). Thomas Hobbes (1588–1679). In http://www.bbc.co.uk/history/historic_figures/hobbes_thomas.shtml. Accessed 07/02/2020

Hobby, E. (1999). *The midwifes book: Jane sharp 1350 to 1850*. Oxford: Oxford University Press.

Hobson, P. (2002). *The cradle of thought: Exploring the origins of thinking*. London: Macmillan.

Holman, B. (2003) in H. Hendrick (2003). *Child welfare: Historical dimensions, contemporary debate*. Bristol: Policy Press.

Holmes, V. (2010). 'My side of the bed': Victorian marriage in the working-class bed. Unpublished paper, given in '*The Body in Bed*' seminar series, History Department, Royal Holloway, University of Holloway.

Holmes, V. (2012). Dangerous spaces: Working-Class homes and fatal household accidents in Suffolk, 1840–1900. Unpublished PhD thesis. Essex: University of Essex.

Holmes, V. (2014). "Death of an infant: Disclosures as to cottage accommodation': Coroners' inquests and the study of Victorian domestic practice. *Home Cultures*. 11(3): 305–31.

Holsinger, V. H., K. T. Rajkowski and J. R. Stabel (1997). Milk pasteurisation and safety: A brief history and update. *Science. Tech*. 16(2): 441–51. In https://www.oie.int/doc/ged/d9152.pdf. Accessed 10/12/2020.

Holt, L. E. (1921). *The care of feeding of children*. London: Vintage Books.

Hopkins, E. (1994). *Childhood transformed: Working-Class children in nineteenth-Century England*. Manchester: Manchester University Press.

Horn, P. (1994). *Children's work and welfare*. Cambridge: Cambridge University Press.

Horn, P. (2019). *The rural world 1780–1850: Social change in the English countryside*. London: Routledge.

Howell, C. (2005). *The foundling museum the foundling*. London: Museum Publications.

Hrdy, S. (1999a). *Mother nature: A history of mothers, infants, and natural selection*. New York: Pantheorn.

Hrdy, S. (1999b). *Mother nature*. London: Chatto and Windus. 697.

Hrdy, S. (2009). *Mothers and others: The evolutionary origins of mutual understanding*. Cambridge, MA: Harvard University Press.

Hrdy, S. (2011). *Mother nature the evolutionary origins of mutual understanding*. London: Harvard University Press.

Humphreys, J. (2010). *Childhood and child labour in the British industrial revolution*. Cambridge: Cambridge University Press.

Iovino, J. (2018). Mother knows best: Parenting tips from Susanna Wesley. In https://www.umc.org/en/content/mother-knows-best-parenting-tips-from-susanna-wesley. Accessed 10/01/2021.

Irvine, D. (2020). *Mary Sumner*. In www.mtbarkeranglicans.org. Accessed 07/09/2020.

Isaacs, S. (1930). *Intellectual growth in young children*. London: Routledge.

Isaacs, S. (1933). *Social development in young children*. London: Routledge.

Isaacs, S. (1951). *Social development in young children*. London: Routledge.

James, A., C. Jenks and A. Prout (2004). *Theorising childhood*. Cambridge: Blackwell.

James, A. and A. Prout (2008). *Constructing and reconstructing childhood*. London: Routledge.

Johnston, J. and L. Nahmad-Williams (2009). *Early childhood studies*. London: Pearson Education.

Kanter, J. (2004). *Face to face children the life and work of Clare Winnicott*. London: Routledge.

Kehily, M. J. (2013). *Understanding childhood a cross disciplinary approach*. Milton Keynes: Open University Press.

Key, E. (1900). *The century of the child*. Milton Keynes: Lightening Source.

Key, E. (2019 [1900]). *Century of the child*. Milton Keynes: Lightning source.

Knott, S. (2019). *Mother*. London: Penguin Books.

Knott, S. (2020). Theorizing and historicizing mothering's many labours. *Past and Present*. 246, Issue Supplement 15: 1–24. In https://doi.org/10.1093/pastj/gtaa032. Accessed 06/03/2021.

Knowles, R. (2020). Carrying matters. In https://www.carryingmatters.co.uk/positive-effects-of-carrying-for-baby/. Accessed 06/03/2021.

Konner, M. (2005). Hunter–gatherer infancy and childhood: The !Kung and others. In M. E. Hewlett, B. S. and M. E. Lamb (Eds.), *Hunter–gatherer childhoods: Evolutionary, developmental, and cultural perspectives*. New Brunswick, NJ: Transaction. 19–64

Kunzel, R. (1993). *Fallen women problem girls*. London: Yale University Press.

Labbok, M. and K. Krasovec (1990). Toward consistency in breastfeeding definitions. *Studies in Family Planning*. 21(4): 226–30. Population Council. Doi:10.2307/1966617

Lancy, D. F. (2014). *The anthropology of childhood: Cherubs, chattel, changelings*. Cambridge: Cambridge University Press.

Landecker, H. (2006). Microcinematography and the history of science and film. *Isis*. 97(1): 121–32.

Larsen, S. F. (1992). Personal context in autobiographical and narrative memories. In M. A. Conway, D. C. Rubin, H. Spinnler and W. A. Wagenaar (Eds.), *Theoretical Perspectives on Autobiographical Memory*. Series D: *Behavioural and Social Sciences*. vol 65. Dordrecht: Springer. https://doi.org/10.1007/978-94-015-7967-4_4

Laslett, P. (1965) in M. Anderson (2007). *Approaches to the history of the western family 1500 to 1914* Cambridge: Cambridge University Press. 10.

Last, N. (2006). *Housewife*. vol 49. London: Profile Books.

Leach, P. (2018). *Transforming infant well-being: Research policy and practice for the first 1001 critical days*. London: Routledge.

Leap, N. and B. Hunter (2013). *A midwifes tale. An oral history from handywomen to professional midwife*. Barnsley Yorkshire: Pen and Sword History.

Lell, E. (nd). *Mothers legacy*. In https://web.archive.org/web/20130930184214/http://www.users.muohio.edu/mandellc/projects/lellem/legacy.htm. Accessed 10/01/2021.

LePlay (nd) in M. Anderson (2007). *Approaches to the history of the western family 1500 to 1914*. Cambridge: Cambridge University Press. 10.

Levine, D. (1987). *Reproducing families: The political economy of England*. Cambridge: Cambridge University Press.

LeVine, R. and R. New (2008). *Anthropology and child development*. Oxford: Blackwell Publishing.

Lilley, I. (1967). *Friedrich Froebel, a selection from his writings*. Cambridge: Cambridge University Press.

Llewellyn Davis, M. (1904). *The women's cooperative guild 1883 to 1904*. Westmoreland: Women's Cooperative Guild.

Llewellyn Davis, M. (2012). *Life as we have known it. London*: Virago Press.

Locke, J. (1689). *The works (an essay concerning human understanding and other writings)*. London: Liberty Fund, Inc. In http://oll.libertyfund.org/titles/locke-the-works-vol-2-an-essay-concerning-human-understanding-part-2-and-other-writings. Accessed 1/11/2019.

Locke, J. (1690). *The works of John Locke (some thoughts concerning education, post-humous works, familiar letters)*. London: Liberty Fund, Inc. In http://oll.libertyfund.org/titles/locke-the-works-vol-8-some-thoughts-concerning-education-posthumous-works-familiar-letters. Accessed 1/11/2019.

Locke, J. (1690). *Essay concerning human understanding*. London: Tegg and Son.

Locke, J. (1693). *Some thoughts concerning education*. London: Tegg and Son.

Locke, J. (2015 [1690]). *Essay concerning human understanding*. London: Sagwan Press.

Lyons, J (1970). *Chomsky*. US: Fontana.

Macintyre, C. (2012). *Understanding babies and young children from conception to three a guide for students, practitioners and parents*. London: Routledge.

Mahood, L. (1980). *Policing, gender, class and family: Britain 1918–1945: A study in social policy development*. London: Routledge.

Mannay, D. (2016). *Visual narratives and creative research methods*. London: Routledge.

Marshall, P. (2009). *The reformation: A very short introduction*. Oxford: Oxford University Press.

Marten, J. (2018). *The history of childhood: A very short introduction*. Oxford: Oxford University Press.

Mass observation (1941). Letter to the local authority maternity and child welfare authorities. Circular 2535 5th December *Joint circular*. In File Reports - Mass Observation Online - Adam Matthew Digital (amdigital.co.uk) Accessed 15/11/2020.

Matthews, M. (2016). The Victorian baby: 19th century advice on motherhood and maternity. In https://www.mimimatthews.com/2016/05/08/the-victorian-baby-19th-century-advice-on-motherhood-and-maternity/ Accessed 15/08/2019.

May, A. N. (1997). 'She at first denied it': Infanticide trials at the old Bailey' in women and history: Voices of early modern England. *Concord*, Ontario: Irwin Publishing. 31–2.

McAlees, M. (2016). UK's '24-hour society' triggers growth in nurseries offering overnight care. In https://www.daynurseries.co.uk/news/article.cfm/id/1576011/A-24-hour-society-creates-demand-for-overnight-childcare Accessed 15/09/2020.

McCarthy, H. (2020a). *Double lives*. London: Bloomsbury.

McCarthy, H. (2020b). Career, family and emotional work: Graduate mothers in 1960s Britain. *Past & Present*. 246, Issue Supplement 15, December 2020: 295–317. https://doi.org/10.1093/pastj/gtaa040

McDonald, D. (2003). The Victorian web: A biography of Collet Woburn Press Home. In www.clara-collet.co.uk. Accessed 27/07/2020.

McIntosh, T. (2017). Changing messages about place of birth in mother and baby magazine between 1956 and 1992. *Midwifery*. 54(1–6). https://doi.org/10.1016/j.midw. 2017.07.017

McMillan, M. (1930). *The nursery school*. Dent: London.

McNamee, S. (2016). *Social study of childhood*. London: Palgrave.

Mead, M. (1928). *Coming of age in Samoa*. New York: William Morrow and Company.

Mead, M. and G. Bateson (1954). Bathing babies in three different cultures [Video file]. In https://www.youtube.com/watch?v=rmvqdDBSY0k Accessed 02/02/2021.

Mickelburgh, J. (2018). Educational pioneers: Susan Isaacs, 1885–1948. In https://eyfs.info/articles.html/teaching-and-learning/educational-pioneers-susan-isaacs-1885-1948-r40/. Accessed 22/07/2019

Miller, L. and C. Cable (1992). *Professionalism in the early years*. London: Hodder Education.

Mills, J. (Ed.) (1999). *Childhood studies: A reader in perspectives of childhood*. London: Routledge.

Mintz, S. (2004). *Huck's raft: A history of American childhood*. Cambridge, MA: Belknap Press.

Montgomery, H. (2009). *An introduction to childhood*. Oxford: Wiley Blackwell.

Moorhead, J. (2015). The Victorian women forced to give up their babies. https://www.theguardian.com/lifeandstyle/2015/sep/19/victorian-women-forced-to-give-up-their-babies-new-exhibition. Accessed 13/10/2020.

Morgan, D. (1996) in S. McNamee (2016). *Social study of childhood*. London: Palgrave.

Moss, P. and P. Pertie (2002). *From children's services to children's spaces: Public policy, children and childhood*. London: Routledge.

Mothers Union (2020). In https://www.mothersunion.org/our-story/our-history. Accessed 17/08/2020.

Muir, A. J. (2017). Courtship, sex and poverty: Illegitimacy in eighteenth-century Wales. *Social History*. 43(1): 56–80. https://doi.org/10.1080/03071022.2018.1394000

Mulley, C. (2019). *The woman who saved the children*. London: Oneworld Publications.

Munro, E. (2011). The Munro review of child protection: Final report a child-centred in system. https://assets.publishing.service.gov.uk/government/uploads/system/uploads/attachment_data/file/175391/Munro-Review.pdf. Accessed 05/09/2020.

Music, G. (2001). *Nurturing natures: Attachment and children's emotional, socio cultural and brain development*. Hove and New York: Psychology Press. 14.

Music, G. (2016). *Nurturing natures: Attachment and children's emotional, socio cultural and brain development*. Hove and New York: Psychology Press. 14.

Myers, k. (1913). Seguin's principles of education as related to the Montessori method. *The Journal of Education*. 77(20) 538–51. http://www.jstor.org/stable/42754542

Nead, L. (2015). The fallen women. In https://foundlingmuseum.org.uk/events/fallen-woman/ Accessed 13/10/2020.

Nead, L (2016). Fallen Women and Foundlings: Rethinking Victorian Sexuality. *History Workshop Journal*. Volume 82, Issue 1, Autumn. Pages 177–187, https://doi.org/10.1093/hwj/dbw040. Accessed 13/10/2020.

Nelson, C. and A. S. Holmes (Eds.) (1997). *Maternal instincts: Visions of motherhood and sexuality in Britain, 1875–1925*. Basingstoke: Ellen Bayuk.

Norman, A. (2019). *From conception to two: Development, policy and practice*. London: Routledge.

QAA Early Childhood Studies, Benchmark statements (2019). In https://www.qaa.ac.uk/docs/qaa/subject-benchmark-statements/subject-benchmark-statement-early-childhood-studies.pdf. 9–10. Accessed 24/04/2021).

Oakley, A. (1981a). *From here to maternity*. London: Penguin Books.

Oakley, A. (1981b). *Becoming a mother*. New York: Schocken Book.

Oakley, A. (1992). *Social support and motherhood*. Oxford: Blackwell.

Oastler, R. (nd). National archives. What did people think of the new Poor Law? In https://www.nationalarchives.gov.uk/education/resources/1834-poor-law/ Accessed 19/09/2020.

Obladen, M. (2014). Pap, gruel, and panada: Early approaches to artificial infant feeding. *Neonatology*. 105(4): 267–74. Doi:10.1159/000357935. PMID: 24577423

Orme, N. (2001). *Mediaeval children*. London, DL: University Press.

Orrock, A. (2019). *Painting childhood*. Warwickshire: Compton Verney Paul Holberton Publishing.

Palmer, S. (2010). *Toxic infanthood: How the modern world is damaging our children and what we can do*. London: Orion.

Parkes, W. (1829). *Domestic duties, or, instructions to young married ladies, on the management of their households, and the regulations of their conduct in the various relations and duties of married life*. United States: J. and J. Harper.

Payne, L. (nd). Infanticide trial transcript from the Old Bailey of Elizabeth Taylor of Clerkenwell, London, June 1734 [Trial Record], in *Children and Youth* in History, Item #162. In https://chnm.gmu.edu/cyh/items/show/162. Accessed 30/1/2021.

Pikler, E. (2018). Guiding principles. In http://thepiklercollection.weebly.com/pikler-principles.html. Accessed 04/10/2018.

Pinker, S. (2004). Why nature and nurture won't go away. *Daedalus*. 133(4): 1–13.

Piper, H. and H. Smith (2003). Touch. *British Educational Research Journal*. 29(6): 879–94, 'Emile [Literary Excerpt],' *in Children and Youth in History*, Item #216. https://chnm.gmu.edu/cyh/items/show/216. Accessed 30/02/2020

Pollard, A. (2005). *Readings for reflective teaching*. London: Continuum.

Pollock, L. (1983). *Forgotten children from 1500 to 1900*. London: Cambridge University Press.

Pollock, L. (1987). *Lasting relationship parents and children over three centuries.* London: London British Library.

Postman, N. (1994) in R. Llorente. Encyclopedia Britannica. In https://www. britannica.com/biography/Neil-Postman. Accessed 29/03/2021.

Pound, L. (2005). *How children learn.* Leamington Spa: Step Forward Publishing.

Rauser, A. (2017). Vitalist statues and the belly pad of 1793. *Journal.* 18(3). In https://www.journal18.org/1373. Doi:10.30610/3.2017.2. Accessed 03/04/2021.

Rawson, B. (nd) in Child's Life Course [Sarcophagus]. Carriage ride, games, death. Rome, early 2nd century CE. Museo Nazionale, Rome. Photo: DAI Rome, 1537. In https://chnm.gmu.edu/cyh/items/show/51 Accessed 30/01/2021.

Read, J. (2019). Maternalist discourse in nursery nurse training at Wellgarth Nursery Training School from 1911 to 1939: Current dilemmas of class and status in historical context. *Gender and Education.* 31(2): 171–88. Doi:10.1080 /09540253.2017.1302076

Rebay-Salisbury, K., J. Dunne, R. B. Salisbury, D. Kern, A. Frisch and R. P. Evershed (2021). Feeding babies at the beginnings of urbanization in central Europe. *Childhood in the Past.* 14(2): 102–24. Doi:10.1080/17585716.2021.1956051

Reed, M and R. Walker (2014). *A critical companion to early childhood.* London: Sage.

Retford, K. (2006). *The art of domestic life family portraiture in 18th century England.* Newhaven, CT and London: Yale University Press.

Roberts, E. (1995a). *Women and families an oral history in 1890 to 1940.* Oxford: Blackwell.

Roberts, E. (1995b). *Woman's place an oral history of working class women 1890 to 1940.* Oxford: Blackwell.

Roberts, E. (1995c). *Women and families an oral history in 1940 to 1970.* Oxford: Blackwell.

Robertson, J. (1958). *Going to hospital with mother* [Film]. United Kingdom: Concord Films.

Robertson, J. and J. Robertson (1969). *Brief separation in infancy: John* [Film]. United Kingdom: Concord Films.

Rogers, G. (2020) John Locke. Encyclopedia Britannica. On Locke, J. (1690) Essay concerning human understanding. In https://www.britannica.com/biography/ John-Locke/An-Essay-Concerning-Human-Understanding Accessed 04/01/20.

Rosmalen, L., R. van der Veer and F. van der Horst (2020). The nature of love: Harlow, Bowlby and Bettelheim on affectionless mothers. *History of Psychiatry.* 31. Doi:10.1177/0957154X19898997. Accessed 16/12/2020.

Ross, E. (1993). *Love and toil motherhood in outcast London 1870 to 1918.* Oxford: Oxford University Press.

Rousseau, J. (1762). *Emile.* London: Pantianos Classics.

Rousseau, J. (1921) *Emile.* Translated by Barbara Foxley. M.A. London and Toronto: J.M. Dent and Sons, New York: E.P. Dutton. In https://oll.libertyfund. org/titles/rousseau-emile-or-education. Accessed 02/03/2021.

Rousseau, J. J. (2011[1762]). *Emile.* London: J.M Dent and Sons.

Rowbotham, S. (1997). *A Century of women.* Middlesex: Viking.

Rowbotham, S. (2011). *Dreamers of a new day.* London: Verso.

Rowold, K. (2019). 'If We Are to Believe the Psychologists … ': Medicine, psychoanalysis and breastfeeding in Britain, 1900–55. *Medical History.* 63(1): 61–81. Doi:10.1017/mdh.2018.63

Running Past (nd). The McMillan Sisters and their Open Air Nursery. In https://runner500.wordpress.com/2015/12/02/the-mcmillan-sisters-and-their-open-air-nursery/. Accessed 22/07/2019.

Rutter, M. (2002). Nature, nurture and development: From Evangelism, through science towards policy and practice. *Child Development*. 73(1): 1–21.

Sagi, A., M. van Ijzendoorn, O. Aviezer, F. Donnell and O. Mayseless (1994). Sleeping out of Home in a Kibbutz communal arrangement: It makes a difference for infant-mother attachment. *Child Development*. 65(4): 992–1004. Doi:10.2307/1131299

Salonen, E., E. Sevón and M. L Laakso (2020). Evening early childhood education and care: Reformulating the institutional culture. *Journal of Early Childhood Research*. 18(4): 418–32. Doi:10.1177/1476718X20947120

Sanchez, M., Ma Cid and R. Lopez (2018). *Motherhood and Infancies is in the Mediterranean in antiquity*. Oxford: Oxbow.

Sandford, J (1966). Cathy come home. In https://www.bbc.com/historyofthebbc/anniversaries/november/cathy-come-home Accessed 22/09/2020.

Sears, W., R. Sears, J. Sears and M., Sears (2006). *The baby sleep book: The complete guide to a good night's rest for the whole family*. New York: Little Brown.

Selby, J. and B. Bradley (2003). Interpreting babies in groups: The ethical imperative. *Human Development*. 46: 197–221.

Seymour (2007) in S. McNamee (2016). *Social study of childhood*. London: Palgrave.

Sharp, J [1671] (1999). *The midwives book or the whole art of widwifry discovered*. Oxford. Oxford University Press.

Sheridan, S. (2021). *Where are the women: A guide to imagined Scotland*. Scotland: Historic Environment.

Sherwin, B. (2007). *Bad medicine*. In https://www.nytimes.com/2007/07/08/books/review/Nuland.html. Accessed 02/03/2021.

Shorter, E. (1976). *Making of the modern family*. London: HarperCollins.

Shpancer, N. (2019). Child of the collective. In https://www.theguardian.com/lifeandstyle/2011/feb/19/kibbutz-child-noam-shpancer. Accessed 13/11/2020.

Simkin (1997). Margaret McMillan. In https://runner500.wordpress.com/2015/12/02/the-mcmillan-sisters-and-their-open-air-nursery/. Accessed 22/07/2019.

Sinclair, A. (2018). *Right from the start*. Paisley: CCWB Press.

Slack, P. (1995a). *The english poor law. 1531–1782*. Cambridge: Cambridge University Press.

Slack, P. (1995b). The poor law. In http://www.workhouses.org.uk/education/. Accessed 28/09/2020.

Smith, K. (2010). *Children and play*. London: Blackwell Publishing.

Smith, L. (1985). *To Understand and to help: The life and work of Susan Isaacs (1885–1948)*. US: Associated University Press.

Sommerville, J. P. (2014). *Politics and Ideology in England, 1603–1640*. London: Routledge London.

Soucy, J. Y. and K. Roth (1997). *Family secrets: The Dionne quintuplets' own story*. New York: Berkeley Books.

Southgate, B. (2000). *Why bother with history?* Harlow: Pearson. 116.

Spiro (1975) in R. LeVine and R. New (2008). *Anthropology and child development*. Oxford: Blackwell Publishing. 143.

Spitz, R. A. (1945). Hospitalism: An enquiry into the genesis of psychiatric conditions in childhood. *The Psychoanalytic Study of the Child.* 1: 53–74.

Spitz, R. A. (1946). Hospitalism: A follow-up report. *The Psychoanalytic Study of the Child.* 2(1): 113–18.

Spock, B. (1945). *The commonsense book of baby and child care.* England: Ishi Press.

Stearns, P. N. (2003). *Anxious parents: A history of modern childrearing in America.* New York: NYU Press.

Stearns, P. N., P. Rowland and L., Giarnella (1999). Children's sleep: Sketching historical change. *Journal of Social History.* 30(2): 345–66.

Stokes, P. (1992). *Norland: The story of the first one hundred years.* Bath: Norland College.

Stone, L. (1979). *The family Sex and marriage, 1500 to 1800.* London: Penguin.

Styles, J. (2010). Threads of feeling. In https://foundlingmuseum.org.uk/events/threads-of-feeling/. Accessed 30/09/2020.

Thompson (1970). in Hendrik, H. (1997). *Children chartered an English society 1880 to 1990.* Cambridge: Cambridge University Press.

Thompson, P. in H. Hendrick (1997). *Children, childhood and English society 1880–1990.* Cambridge: Cambridge University Press. 18.

Tilghman, C. (2003). Autobiography as dissidence: Subjectivity, sexuality, and the women's co-operative guild. *Biography.* 26(4): 583–606. Accessed 05/04/2021. In http://www.jstor.org/stable/23540443

Tinbergen, N. (1963) in S. Hrdy (1999). *Mother nature.* London: Chatto and Windus. 697.

Tizard, B. (1977). *Adoption: A second chance.* London: Open Books.

Tovey, H. (2012). *Bringing the Frobel approach to your early years setting.* London: Routledge.

Trevarthen, C. (1993). Predispositions to cultural learning in young infants. *Behavioral and Brain Sciences.* 16(3): 534–5.

Trevarthen, C. (2001). Intrinsic motives for companionship in understanding: Their origin development and their significance for mental health. *Infant Mental Health Journal.* 22: 95–131.

van der Horst, F., H. A LeRoy and R. van der Veer (2008). 'When strangers meet': John Bowlby and Harry Harlow on attachment behavior. *Integrative Psychological and Behavioral Science.* 42: 370–88.

Vargo, G. (2017). *An underground history of early Victorian fiction: Chartism, radical print culture, and the social problem novel.* Cambridge Studies in Nineteenth-Century Literature and Culture. Cambridge: Cambridge University Press. Doi:10.1017/9781108181891

Violett, A. (2018a). Influences on affection and discipline in late nineteenth and early twentieth century parent-child relationships. In https://histperspectives.wordpress.com/histper-blog/influences-on-affection-and-discipline-in-late-nineteenth-and-early-twentieth-century-parent-child-relationships/. Accessed 15/12/2020.

Violett, A. (2018b). The public perceptions and personal experiences of only children growing up in Britain, c. 1850–1950. Thesis. Essex University. In http://repository.essex.ac.uk/22943/1/alice-violett-final-thesis.pdf. Accessed 16/12/2020.

Wade and Smart (2002) in S. McNamee (2016). *Social study of childhood.* London: Palgrave. 94.

Walker, I. (2018). Bedrooms of London. In https://foundlingmuseum.org.uk/events/bedrooms-of-london/ Accessed 22/10/2020.

Watson, J. B. and R. A. Watson (1928). *Psychological care of infant and child*. New York: Norton.

Watson, R. A. (2021). René Descartes. Encyclopedia Britannica. In https://www.britannica.com/biography/Rene-Descartes. Accessed 05/04/2021. http://www.unionhistory.info/matchworkers/matchworkers.php

Wenke, R. (1990). *Patterns in prehistory: Humankind's first three million*. Oxford: Oxford University Press.

Whitbread, N. (1972). *The evolution of nursery infant schools*. London: Routledge.

White, E. J. (2009). Bakhtinian dialogism: A philosophical and methodological route to dialogue and difference? *Annual Conference of the Philosophy of Education Society of Australasia*. In http://www2.hawaii.edu/~pesaconf/zpdfs/16white.pdf. Accessed 16/12/2020.

White, J. (2015). *Introducing dialogic pedagogy: Provocations for the early years*. London: Routledge.

Wilkinson, E. J (2006). Early years Pioneers: Jean-Jacques Rousseau. In https://www.nurseryworld.co.uk/features/article/early-years-pioneers-jean-jacques-rousseau. Accessed 14/11/2020.

Wilson, A. (1980). The infancy of the history of childhood: An appraisal of Philippe Aries. *History and Theory*. 19(2): 132–53.

Winnicott, D. W. (1964). *The child, the family and the outside world*. London: Penguin.

Winnicott, D. W. and C. Britton (1957). Residential management as treatment for difficult children. In D. W. Winnicott (Ed.), *The child and the outside world: studies in developing relationships*. London: Tavistock.

Wokler, R. (1995). *Rousseau a short introduction*. Oxford: Oxford University Press.

Wolf, J. (1999). 'Mercenary Hirelings' or 'A Great Blessing'?: Doctors' and mothers' conflicted perceptions of wet nurses and the ramifications for infant feeding in Chicago, 1871–1961. *Journal of Social History*. 33(1): 97–120. In https://www.jstor.org/stable/3789462?mag=lifesaving-horrifying-history-wet-nurses&seq=1#metadata_info_tab_contents. Accessed 03/04/2021.

Worth, J. (2005). *Shadows of the workhouse*. London: Orion.

Wright, H. R. (2015). *The Child in society*. London: Sage.

Wright, P. (1987). The social construction of babyhood: The definition of infant care as a medical problem. In A. Bryman, B. Bytheway, P. Allatt, T. Keil (Eds.), *Rethinking the life cycle: Explorations in sociology*. London: Palgrave Macmillan. https://doi.org/10.1007/978-1-349-18919-9_7. Accessed 16/12/2020.

Wrigley, E. and R. Schofield (1983). English population history from family reconstitution: Summary results 1600–1799. *Population Studies*. 37(2): 157–84. Doi:10.2307/2173980.

Zeedyk, S. (2008). Brain development. In http://www.suzannezeedyk.com/category/brain_development/ Accessed 13/01/2021.

https://www.thekeep.info/. Accessed. 13/01/2021

http://www.barbarakatzrothman.com/2021/01/. Accessed 11/10/2020

INDEX